Contents

Acknowledgments *v*

Introduction *vii*

The Quiz *viii*

1 National Firsts *1*
2 Chicago Firsts *5*
3 The Good Guys *12*
4 Notorious and Nefarious Characters *17*
5 Bricks and Mortar *25*
6 By Any Other Name *35*
7 Playtime *41*
8 All the News That's Fit to Print *49*
9 Says Who? *52*
10 All That Jazz *54*
11 Street Signs *58*
12 We Got Class *69*
13 Catastrophes *76*
14 Star Gazing *79*

15 Gone, but Not Forgotten 90
16 The Political Machine 92
17 Big Business 97
18 Animals 104
19 Athletes' Feats 107
20 By Land, Sea, or Air 118
21 The Neighborhoods 126
22 What's Cooking in Chicago Kitchens 129
23 Law and Order 139
24 Some Windy City Weather 143
25 World Records 146
26 Cocktail Party Tidbits 152

Index 157

Dolores A. Long

Contemporary Books, Inc.
Chicago

Library of Congress Cataloging in Publication Data

Long, Dolores A.
   The Chicago trivia book.

   Includes index.
   1. Chicago (Ill.)—History—Miscellanea.
I. Title.
F548.35.L66   1982   977.3'11   82-45406
ISBN 0-8092-5690-8

> This book is dedicated to my parents, Robert and Helen Long; my sisters, Loretta Long Varley and Rosemary Long; and my friend Artemus—because they know me best of all, and have loved me even when the going got rough.

Copyright © 1982 by Dolores A. Long
All rights reserved
Published by Contemporary Books, Inc.
180 North Michigan Avenue, Chicago, Illinois 60601
Manufactured in the United States of America
Library of Congress Catalog Card Number: 82-45406
International Standard Book Number: 0-8092-5690-8

Published simultaneously in Canada by
Beaverbooks, Ltd.
150 Lesmill Road
Don Mills, Ontario M3B 2T5
Canada

Acknowledgments

Research assistance in the preparation of this book was provided by the *Chicago Tribune;* the *Sun-Times;* the Chicago Public Library; the Chicago Municipal Reference Library; *Chicago;* the Chicago Historical Society; *Vittles and Vice,* by Patricia Bronte; Lettuce Entertain You Enterprises; *Lords of the Levee,* by Lloyd Wendt and Herman Kogan; *Mayors, Madams, and Madmen,* by Norman Mark; *People to See,* by Jay Robert Nash; *The Germans of Chicago,* by Rudolph A. Hofmeister; *Black Chicago: The Making of a Negro Ghetto,* by Allan H. Spear; *Old Chicago Houses,* by John Drury; *500 Things to Do in Chicago for Free,* by Jim Hargrove and Patrick K. Snook; *Norman Mark's Chicago,* by Norman Mark; *Italians in Chicago 1880–1930: A Study in Ethnic Nobility,* by Humbert S. Nelli; *Who Runs Chicago?* by Michael Kilian, Connie Fletcher, and F. Richard Ciccone; *A Kid's Guide to Chicago,* by Jerry Nelson; *Chicago: Growth of a Metropolis,* by Harold M. Mayer and Richard C. Wade; The Chicago Convention and Tourism Bureau; and Festivals, Inc. A special thank you, as well, to Jody Rein.

Introduction

Why a book on Chicago trivia? Because it's the little things in life that tend to pique our interest, stir our curiosity, or just plain stick in our minds when all the book learning and memorized facts fade away into the distance.

When I first came to Chicago, I found myself constantly asking others, "Why this? Who's that? Do you know if, when, and how?" I started to clip and save every newspaper and magazine article I came across that spotlighted the city's unknown heroes and little-known facets. I found these articles fascinating, and I found that they gave me a keener appreciation for the city, its people, and its history.

My fascination with the intriguing bits of information that make up the whole picture of Chicago resulted in this book. It by no means contains every piece of trivia that can be culled from the city's history, but instead, those I thought would provide the most interesting reading. So much of life is serious and rather sad. I like to think that concentrating on trivia now and then helps give us a balanced perspective—life is meant to be joyous and frivolous at times, too!

Dolores A. Long
Chicago, 1982

The Quiz

So, you think you know Chicago? The following quiz is just a sampling of the facts, foibles, travesties, and tidbits contained in *The Chicago Trivia Book.**

Score 0 to 5: You're a tourist, a neophyte resident, or hey, you'd better start reading!
Score 5 to 10: You know the lake is always east, you know your own neighborhood, but you'd probably get lost driving on lower Wacker Drive.
Score 11 to 15: You've been spending some time at the Chicago Historical Society!
Score 16 to 19: Don't hesitate to apply for a job at the Visitor and Information Bureau.
Perfect Score: You either cheated, or you're Henry, my research assistant.

---

*For those of you who like seeing all the answers at one shot, see page 156.

The Quiz

1. Who was the engineer responsible for reversing the flow of the Chicago River? (See page 124.)
2. What Chicago coach wrote America's first book on football? (See p. 2.)
3. What political post did social reformer Jane Addams once hold? (See p. 13.)
4. What is a Chicago typewriter? (See p. 18.)
5. How did Mobster Dion O'Banion disguise his illegal bootleg operations? (See p. 23.)
6. What city park was originally a city dump? (See p. 26.)
7. What popular amusement park attraction made its debut at the Chicago World's Fair in 1893? (See p. 42.)
8. What's a Blind Pig? (See p. 19.)
9. Who coined the phrase, "There's a sucker born every minute?" (See p. 53.)
10. What romantic tradition began at Chicago's Everleigh Club? (See p. 80.)
11. What is July 11th in Chicago? (See p. 91.)
12. What landmark Chicago building was purchased for $14 million in 1945, sight unseen? (See p. 100.)
13. What sweet-tooth pleaser did "Candy Man" Charles Gunther invent? (See p. 36.)
14. What movie Tarzan began his career at the Illinois Athletic Club? (See p. 111.)
15. What did the call letters WGN and WLS originally stand for? (See p. 88.)
16. Which Chicago skyscraper houses the highest swimming pool in the world? (See p. 147.)
17. What is the oldest ball park in the major leagues? (See p. 149.)
18. What Chicagoan is credited with being America's first woman detective? (See p. 141.)
19. When was the coldest day in Chicago on record? (See p. 145.)
20. How much do shoppers spend annually at Water Tower Place? (See p. 153.)

1

National Firsts

Chicago receives the epithet "Second City" from the Bureau of the Census population statistics. For all those residents who are irked by connotations of second place or runner-up status, the following chapter offers just a few of the many occasions when Chicago shone first in the limelight. You will find a wide variety of other Second City firsts to brag about throughout this book; here are some to get you started.

2   THE CHICAGO TRIVIA BOOK

The first book on football, complete with play diagrams, was written by Chicago coach Amos Alonzo Stagg and Dr. Henry Williams in 1893.

The first baseball team in the nation to attend spring training was the Chicago White Stockings in 1886. The team traveled to Hot Springs, Arkansas, to enjoy the therapeutic baths.

The "Mickey Finn," knockout powder mixed with a cocktail, was invented in Chicago by Lone Star Saloon operator Mickey Finn in 1896. It was a convenient way to drug customers and roll them for their money.

Alexander Graham Bell made the first long-distance telephone call between New York and Chicago in 1892. Bell, in New York, called Chicago's mayor. The phone used for this historic occasion is now housed in Illinois Bell's Telephone Museum at 225 West Randolph.

Chicago's Jay Berwanger was the first Heisman Trophy winner in 1935.

Batter up! The first regulation baseballs and bats used by professional players were manufactured by Chicago entrepreneur (and former pitcher) Albert G. Spalding.

The Home Insurance Building at LaSalle and Adams, built by Maj. William LeBaron Jenney in 1885, was the first building in the nation to use the Chicago skeleton method of construction, in which the steel frame supports the weight of the building.

Rush Street was the site of the first iron bridge built in the Midwest, in 1856.

In 1884, the first buffalo ever born in captivity was born at the Lincoln Park Zoo.

Chicago produced the first:

steel frame skyscraper
stainless steel building
electric iron and cooking range
Pullman railroad car
grain reaper
reactor to produce electricity from atomic energy
cafeteria
zipper fastener
elevated railway
window envelope
two-pants suit of clothes

Paris-born Ahlyce Kaplan is the country's first female full-charge concierge. She caters to the whims and wants of celebrities staying at the Whitehall Hotel.

Chicagoan Barbara Proctor is the first black woman in the United States to own and operate an advertising agency, Proctor & Gardner Advertising.

The Tiffany mosaic dome, located between the sixth and seventh floors of Marshall Field's State Street store, was designed and built under the direction of the master himself, Louis C. Tiffany. The dome is the largest glass mosaic with an unbroken surface in the country, with six thousand square feet and one thousand pieces of glass. Fifty men labored for a year and a half to install the elegant showpiece.

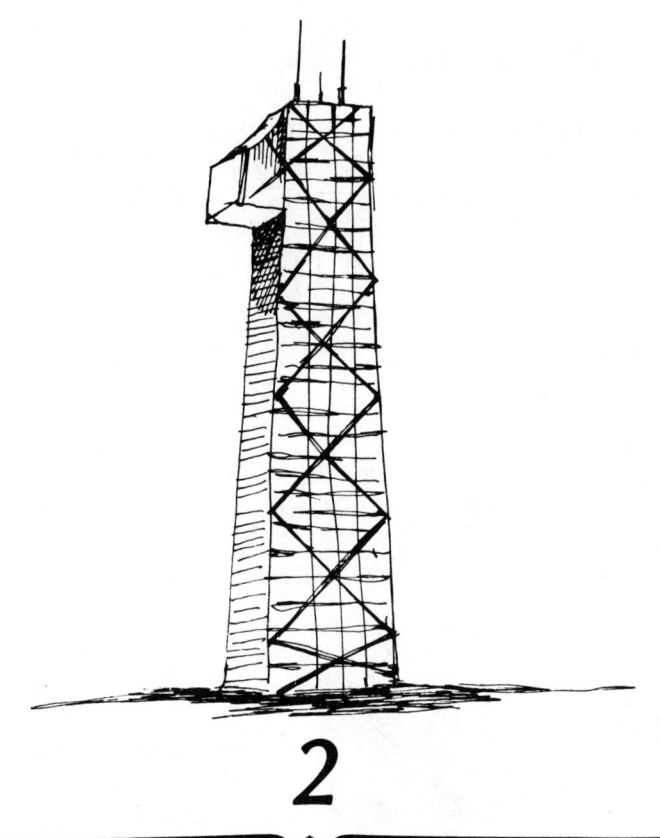

2

Chicago Firsts

Chicago may be the nation's second-place city in terms of population, but there are plenty of historical city firsts to balance the scales.

Here are enough firsts from Chicago's own history to keep you winning obscure bets for weeks.

6   THE CHICAGO TRIVIA BOOK

The city's first hotelier was Mark Beaubien, who built (1829) and served as host of the Eagles Exchange Tavern at Lake and Wacker. Beaubien renamed his establishment the Sauganash Inn, in 1832, after his friend Billy Caldwell, an Indian chief whose tribal name was Sauganash.

The elections of May 2, 1837, put William B. Ogden into office as the city's first mayor.

Chicago's first citizen, Jean-Baptiste Pointe du Sable, was a black fur trader who established a trading post at the mouth of the Chicago River with his Potawatomi Indian wife. The trading post was later sold to silversmith John Kinzie.

Jean-Baptiste kept firsts in the family. The first birth on record in Chicago was that of his daughter, Eulalia, in 1796.

The city's first chief engineer, Ellis S. Chesbrough, put a stop to the citizenry using Lake Michigan as a toilet by designing Chicago's sewer system.

John Wellborn Root supervised the construction of Chicago's first "skyscraper," the sixteen-story Monadnock Building at 53 West Jackson Boulevard, in 1891.

The first public building in Chicago was erected in 1832 at a cost of twelve dollars, an estray pen built to contain the hogs and cattle roaming about the area.

The first man to be jailed in Chicago was Richard Harper, who listed his occupation as "loafer."

BATTER UP!

Potter Palmer served as the first president of the Chicago Baseball Club.

Your Guide to the Palmer House

SCHOOL DAZE

The first schoolteacher in Chicago, John Watkins, immigrated to the city in 1832.

IS THERE A DOCTOR IN THE HOUSE?

The first antiseptic surgery in Chicago was performed at Cook County Hospital by Dr. Christian Fenger in the 1870s; Otto Schmidt introduced the first x-ray machine in the city in 1893.

The first surgical procedure on record in the city took place in 1832, when Dr. Elijah Harmon amputated the frozen foot of a mail carrier.

HARD WORKERS

Chicago is the city that works, and the following men were first to do so in their field:

iron manufacturer: Clemens Stose
brewers: Michael Lill and Michael Diversey
brickmaker: Heinrich Lampmann
professional musician: Nicholas Berdell
grave digger: Heinrich Gherken
cafe owner: Frederick Burky

Fur trader Guerdon Hubbard was Chicago's first insurance underwriter and its first banker, and he built the city's first brick building.

BUT NO MARTINIS

Joseph "Chesterfield Joe" Mackin is credited with starting the custom of a free lunch in Chicago by giving customers a free oyster with every beer. Alas, the free lunch has gone the way of the three-martini lunch.

Chicago's first public school was opened by Miss Eliza Chappel in a general store located on Wacker Drive between State and Dearborn streets in 1833.

The first home to burn in Chicago's Great Fire of 1871 was that of James Dalton, neighbor to the Patrick O'Learys, whose cow allegedly set the blaze.

Chicago Firsts

The first Chicago post office was in the log cabin store of John S. C. Hogan near Lake and Wacker. Mail was delivered from the East once a week in 1833.

The city's first fire company was founded in 1835 after a meeting in Ike Cook's saloon on South Water Street.

The first animal bought for the Lincoln Park Zoo was a bear cub, purchased for $10 on June 1, 1874. The zoo's second major purchase didn't occur until 1877—two bears, two peafowl, a kangaroo, a condor, and a goat, all for $275.

Chicago's first Gold Coast neighborhood was located between the 1600 and 2200 blocks of Prairie Avenue.

Weary shoppers gave their tootsies a rest when the first escalators in the city were installed at Marshall Field's department store in 1933 as a salute to Chicago's Century of Progress Exposition.

The first steam fire engine in Chicago was named *Long John* in honor of Chicago's Mayor "Long John" Wentworth.

The first tunnel to draw drinking water from Lake Michigan was completed in 1867. It was two miles in length and had been dug through sixty feet of clay under the lake bed.

The first railroad to be built in Chicago, the Galena and Chicago Union, was constructed to connect the city with the lead mines in Galena. *The Pioneer* was the first locomotive to arrive in Chicago from Galena, in 1848.

10 THE CHICAGO TRIVIA BOOK

Chicago's first railroad terminal, the Galena and Chicago Union Depot, was located at Canal and Kinzie streets between the years 1848 and 1853.

The first elevated railroad in Chicago was introduced in 1892, running from the downtown area as far south as Thirty-ninth Street, and it was extended to Jackson Park in time for the World's Columbian Exposition of 1893.

Chicago Historical Society

The first brand of Wrigley's chewing gum on the market was called Vassar, named after the tiny New England women's college. Next off the assembly line was Lotta (as in "gotta have a lot of") and Sweet Sixteen Orange, the forerunner of Juicy Fruit.

The first Chicago public school to offer gymnastics in the curriculum was West Side German High School, in 1871.

GIMME THAT OL' TIME RELIGION

Chicago is populated by people who follow virtually every religious persuasion, and weekly church attendance is an important part of life in the city today.

The first Catholic mass in Chicago was said by Father John Saint Cyr in the home of innkeeper Mark Beaubien. Father John was also the first pastor of the city's first Catholic church, Saint Mary's. The church was erected in 1833 at the southwest corner of State and Lake.

Chicago's first resident clergyman was François Pinet, who founded the Guardian Angel Mission in 1696 in the North Loop area.

Arthur B. Meeker took a bride in the first church wedding held in Chicago. The nuptials occurred September 24, 1856, in the LaSalle Street Baptist Church.

The first Roman Catholic Eucharistic Congress ever held in America took place in Chicago in 1926.

The first black church in Chicago, Quinn Chapel African Methodist Episcopal at 2401 South Wabash Avenue, opened its doors in 1847.

3

The Good Guys

Although it's become fashionable in the news to focus on what's wrong with the world and to glamorize criminal activity, there still are and always have been a hundred hard workers for every rotten apple.

No, they don't all wear white hats. But through their benevolence, generosity, foresight, and sacrifice, Chicago is a much richer place.

AWARD WINNERS

Chicago's own Jane Addams, founder of Hull House, was the first American woman to win the Nobel Prize for Peace (1931). Jane Addams, by the way, who opened Hull House in 1889 to aid Chicago immigrants, was once garbage inspector of the city's Nineteenth Ward.

The first American scientist to receive the Nobel Prize in physics was Albert Abraham Michelson, head of the physics department at the University of Chicago.

BENEFACTORS

Dr. Charles Dyer headed the Underground Railroad effort in Chicago during the mid-nineteenth century, when public sentiment ran high against returning slaves who had escaped from the South.

Mail order magnate Aaron Montgomery Ward became known as "the Watchdog of the Lakefront" for his support of an 1836 legal provision for "public ground forever to remain vacant of building" along the city's lakefront, an act that made possible the creation of Grant Park.

Chicago Convention and Tourism Bureau

14   THE CHICAGO TRIVIA BOOK

Senator Stephen A. Douglas donated several acres of land to start the first Chicago university.

In 1917, Sears, Roebuck executive Julius Rosenwald established the Rosenwald Fund to aid Chicago's black population and funded Booker T. Washington's Tuskegee Institute with a $2.5 million gift.

Bishop Bernard Sheil founded the Golden Gloves boxing program in Chicago as a means to combat juvenile delinquency during the Great Depression.

English novelist Thomas Hughes is known as "the Father of the Chicago Public Library" for helping to organize a large donation of books from England's Queen Victoria to seed the city's first library.

THE FATHER OF HYDE PARK

Paul Cornell is honored as "the Father of Hyde Park." In 1867, Cornell aided in having the state legislature pass the South Parks Bill, allocating the use of certain lands for boulevards and parks. Jackson and Washington parks and the Midway Plaisance were formed from this land.

HEROES

Col. Elmer E. Ellsworth was the first Chicagoan to die in the Civil War.

Kasper Lauer was the first police officer to die in the line of duty, on September 18, 1854.

David Kenison, a member of colonial America's Boston Tea Party, is buried in Lincoln Park at Clark and Wisconsin, honored by a simple memorial marker.

Mayor "Big Bill" Thompson was hailed as "the Man Who Put the Sun in Sunday" for enforcing the blue laws against Sunday liquor sales in the city.

"Spider" Dan Goodwin managed to climb both the Sears Tower and the John Hancock Building in 1981 despite police and fire department efforts to thwart his acrobatics, cheered on by crowds below. He has since become a social climber, advertising men's formal wear.

HOT LIPS!

Lt. Richard Pierson Hobson, a hero of the Spanish-American War, set a new record when he visited Chicago with Adm. George Dewey and kissed 163 women in one evening, averaging 4.444 kisses per minute.

R.I.P

Prominent millionaire brewmaster Peter Shoenhofen was laid to rest in style, buried in a pyramid mausoleum in Graceland Cemetery.

Three Chicago parks are named in honor of three assassinated U.S. presidents: Lincoln, Garfield, and McKinley.

To honor his final wishes to be buried in Chicago, the body of Newberry Library founder Walter Newberry was sealed in a cask of rum to preserve it during an ocean voyage from France to Chicago for burial.

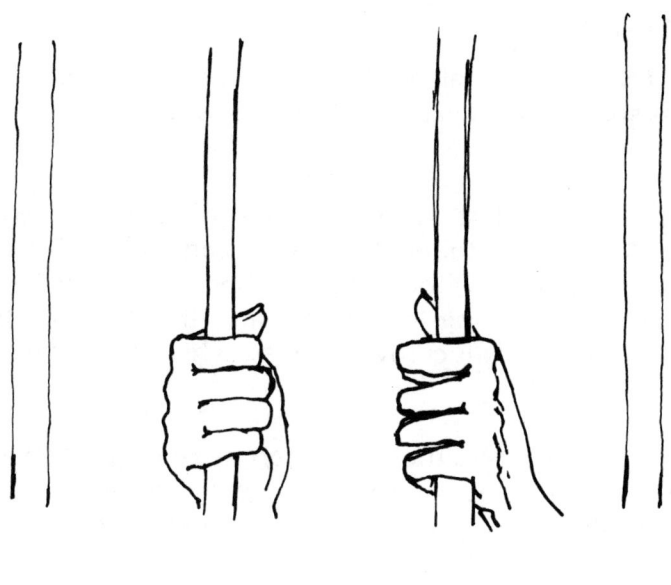

4

Notorious and Nefarious Characters

Hollywood and the news media have so glamorized the activities of Chicago's syndicate hoodlums of the Roaring Twenties that most of the United States and many international visitors immediately conjure up visions of Capone, machine guns, and Eliot Ness whenever Chicago is mentioned.

The chronicles of Chicago's gangster era contain such exciting characters and interesting events that it's small wonder they are still the subject of much conversation and fascination even in the late twentieth century.

TAKE COVER

Dion O'Banion organized Chicago's first syndicate with the able assistance of "Nails" Morton and Johnny Torrio.

During the stormiest years of Chicago's gangster era, September 1923 to October 1926, approximately 215 gangsters were slain by other hoods and another 160 gunned down by the law, as the gangsters made an all-out effort to gain control of the city's lucrative bootleg whiskey business.

Gangster activity became so brazen at one point that Antonio Lombardo, head of the Unione Sicilione, was gunned down in 1928 at the city's busiest street corner, State and Madison, at midday.

Citizens ran for cover when they heard the rat-a-tat of the "Chicago typewriter," another name for the submachine gun.

Gangland justice in Chicago was swift: Informants were murdered with a bullet in the throat, and mobsters who worked both sides of the law had their "two faces" blown away.

PUBLIC ENEMY

Public Enemy No. 1 John Dillinger bought frogs' legs at Ireland's Restaurant every night for six weeks prior to meeting his destiny at the Biograph Theatre. Obviously, frogs' legs aren't lucky.

Notorious and Nefarious Characters   19

Dillinger met with an FBI slug when the infamous Lady in Red betrayed him to the Feds in the alley next to the Biograph Theatre, 2433 North Lincoln Avenue, on July 22, 1934.

Gangster Johnny Torrio is credited with dividing the city into "districts" to control the more than eight hundred mobsters jockeying for power within the city.

DON'T TAKE ANY WOODEN ONES

Nineteenth Ward boss Johnny Powers drew votes by throwing nickels to schoolchildren in the neighborhood and handing out cigars to the voters.

KING OF THE BROTHELS

Ike Bloom operated Freiberg Hall on a round-the-clock basis. The hall was a hangout where prostitutes met their customers at night but where official political business meetings were held during the day.

AIN'T WE GOT FUN

Mobster Al Capone maintained a torture dungeon under his Four Deuces Saloon at 2222 South Wabash Avenue.

SPEAKEASY

Blind Pigs was a popular name for an illegal saloon in the Toddlin' Town.

Marge's Bar at 1758 North Sedgwick was once an ice cream parlor disguising a speakeasy.

By 1923, Chicago had 6,500 illegal saloons, which Mayor William Dever, much to the dismay of many citizens, promptly labeled as "vicious cabarets" and vowed to close down.

BOOTLEGGERS

The "Dry Sunday" law of 1915 prohibited the sale of liquor on Sundays. Capt. George Wellington Streeter (of Streeterville fame) nevertheless continued to sell beer in his Chestnut Street soft drink parlor. A confrontation with the police and a shooting incident soon forced the ornery tavern owner to shut down.

The most notorious peddlers of bootlegged beer during the Roaring Twenties were Johnny Torrio and his lieutenant, "Scarface" Al Capone. Torrio and Capone cleared some $30 million annually from the sale of bootlegged hooch.

Chicago Historical Society, Rogue's Gallery Portrait, 1931. DN# 94, 945

Notorious and Nefarious Characters

HIT MEN

Frank McErlane is credited as being the first mobster to use the submachine gun during the 1920s bootleg wars.

Gangster Hymie Weiss is said to have invented the phrase "take him for a ride."

WHO WAS THAT?

Kingpin Al Capone often used business cards that claimed he was Al Brown, used furniture dealer.

Los Angeles gangster Mickey Cohen once hid out at the Drake Hotel and registered under the name of radio private eye character Martin Kane. Evicted when one of the front desk clerks recognized his true identity, Cohen took his baggage up the street to the Ambassador East, where police promptly nabbed him.

NICKNAMES

Capone's nickname among friends and foes alike was "Big Fellow."

Michael "Hinky Dink" Kenna earned his nickname from his short stature—five feet, four inches.

Local newspapers dubbed Capone "the Mayor of Crook County" because of his influence at City Hall.

Street brawler or war hero? "Scarface" Al Capone claimed to have received his facial scars fighting in France, but in truth he had been cut during a row with a Brooklyn barber.

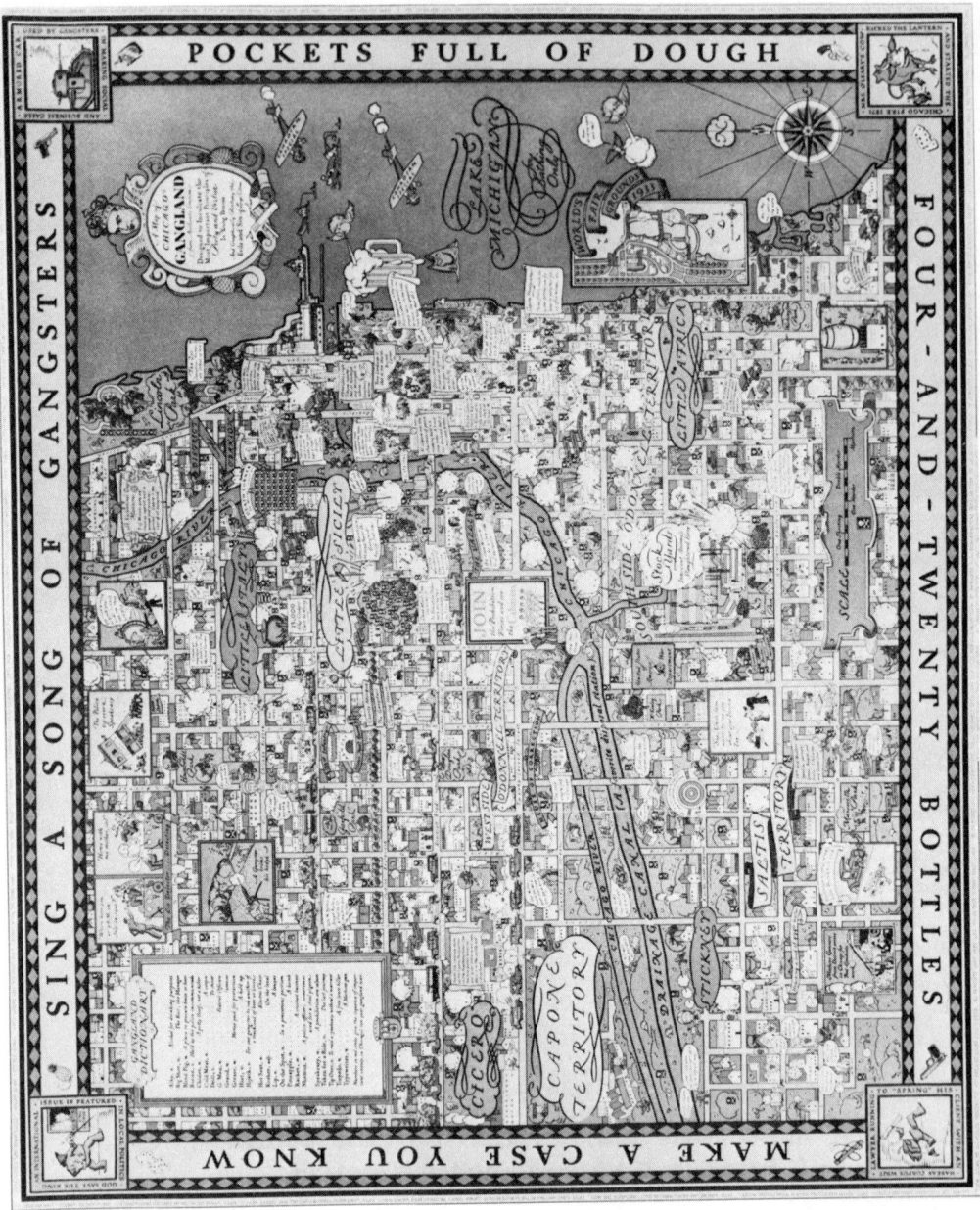
Chicago Historical Society

HEARTS AND FLOWERS

Mobster Dion O'Banion disguised his illegal bootleg operation as a flower shop on State Street, located across from the Holy Name Cathedral.

The most celebrated day in the chronicles of Chicago's gangster activity was the Saint Valentine's Day Massacre in 1929. Five men masquerading as policemen gunned down seven members of the "Bugs" Moran gang in a garage at 2122 North Clark. Ironically, George "Bugs" Moran was the only member of his gang to survive this hit.

SUCH LUCK

Hymie Weiss tried to assassinate Al Capone by using eleven automobiles armed with men shooting more than one thousand bullets at Capone's Hawthorne Inn headquarters in Cicero. Luckily for Capone, he was hungry and had gone next door to eat. He escaped the incident unharmed.

Al Capone's downtown headquarters occupied fifty rooms on two floors of the Hotel Metropole on South Michigan Avenue, guarded day and night by armed gunmen.

TOO MANY FLOWERS

Dion O'Banion was the first mobster to die in Chicago's gangster wars. His funeral cortege included twenty-six truckloads of flowers, including a basket of roses "From Al."

Dion's "late" gift wasn't unique. To reinforce his alibi of always being somewhere else when a rival mobster was murdered, Al Capone always sent an impressive wreath of flowers to the funeral, with a card reading "From Al." It was not uncommon for Capone to spend several thousand dollars for a public display of "grief."

LAW AND ORDER?

"The Sands," a popular red-light district next to the river, was set ablaze by Maj. John Wentworth in 1860 in an attempt to rid the city of vice. The effects of this noble effort failed to last very long.

Of the more than one thousand gangland murders on record in Chicago since 1919, only four gangsters have ever been convicted.

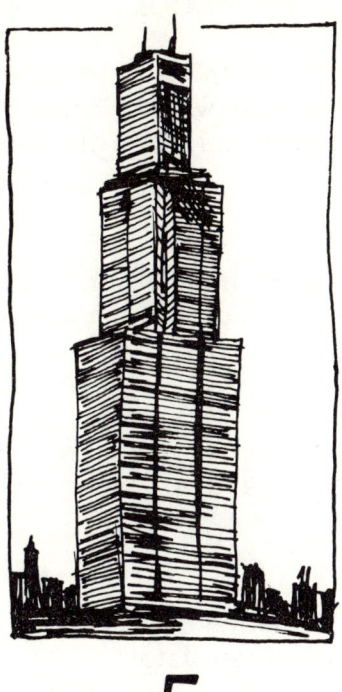

5

Bricks and Mortar

The physical appearance of Chicago has evolved from flat, muddy prairie land to a skyline that boasts the world's first- and fourth-tallest buildings. As home base for such architectural geniuses as Frank Lloyd Wright, Chicago has established itself as a focal point of architectural innovation.

House moving was a common practice in the early days of Chicago. Wealthy homeowners often had their houses wheeled off to better locations in the city that caught their fancy.

Chicago's oldest house, built around 1836, is the Henry B. Clarke residence at 1855 South Indiana Avenue.

GOING UP?

Fifty elevators and five escalators in the John Hancock Building transport more than twelve thousand passengers daily.

The Chicago Marriott Hotel on Michigan Avenue houses the city's only four-story-tall escalator.

ALMOST A CITY IN ITSELF

The Merchandise Mart covers two entire city blocks and has a seven hundred-page directory of tenants.

GOOD USE OF GARBAGE

Grant Park was originally a landfill made from the refuse of the business district after the Chicago Fire.

THE BUILDING THAT NEVER WAS

In 1956, Frank Lloyd Wright proposed construction of the "Illinois," a 5,280-foot building near the Adler Planetarium to house 130,000 office workers. Wright needed a paltry $100 million to finance his pie-in-the-sky idea, but he had no takers.

MEET ME UNDER THE CLOCK

Long a convenient meeting landmark for downtown shoppers, the first of Marshall Field's big clocks was installed at the corner of Washington and State on November 26, 1897. The cast bronze clock, mounted some 17½ feet above the sidewalk, weighs a hefty 7¾ tons.

Chicago Convention and Tourism Bureau

THE BUILDING DESIGNED BY A CONTEST

In 1923, the *Chicago Tribune* sponsored a competition to design its new Michigan Avenue headquarters. It was won by Howells and Hood, who garnered $100,000 for their drawing.

Chicago Tribune

Tribune Tower may be home for the *Chicago Tribune*, but its exterior walls boast pieces of other famous buildings that are more than a stone's throw away from Chicago. Embedded in the Tribune Tower's walls are authentic stones from Westminster Abbey, the Alamo, Hamlet's castle, the Great Pyramid, the Taj Mahal, Fort Sumter, and the Arc de Triomphe.

SKYSCRAPERS

Lake Point Tower at 70 stories (640 feet) is the tallest apartment building in the city.

Water Tower Place at 74 stories (871 feet) is the tallest reinforced concrete building in Chicago.

Bricks and Mortar 29

The all-electric John Hancock Center at 875 North Michigan Avenue was constructed with 46,000 tons of steel, 1,250 miles of wiring, and 11,459 window panes. It stands as the tallest building in the world used for office, commercial, and residential purposes.

Chicago Convention and Tourism Bureau

The 62-story twin spires of Marina City, constructed in 1964, comprise the tallest concrete building in the city using no structural steel.

THE CHICAGO TRIVIA BOOK

Chicago Convention and Tourism Bureau

CHEWING GUM HEADQUARTERS

The Wrigley Building's landmark clock tower is patterned after the Giralda Tower in Spain.

Under instructions from William Wrigley, architects designed the Wrigley Building to look like "a luscious birthday cake."

ROOM AND BOARD

Chicago is home to the first totally fireproofed hotel, the Palmer House at State and Monroe. After the original structure burned to the ground in the Great Fire of 1871, the owners decided not to take any chances in securing the second building from the same fate, and they built the new hotel completely out of brick and iron.

The first Palmer House before the fire - 1871

Your Guide to the Palmer House

To complete the building on schedule, builders worked twenty-four hours a day to construct the Palmer House hotel, using calcium light and gas flares to work by night.

Palmer House 1873 to 1924

The Radisson Hotel was originally the Medinah Athletic Club, offering a twenty-five–yard swimming pool on its sixteenth floor, which is still open to hotel guests and the public.

LOTS OF ELBOW GREASE . . .

And six automatic window-washing machines clean the 110 stories of windows on the Sears Tower eight times a year.

THE FASTEST-BUILT BUILDING IN CHICAGO

The Wigwam, located at the corner of Lake and Market streets, was constructed in a record five weeks to open in time for the Republican Convention of 1860, at a cost of $5,000.

IT'S A BIRD, IT'S A PLANE . . .

No, it's the light atop the Playboy Building, known as the Lindbergh Beacon, shining with an intensity of two billion candles.

DOCTORS' DWELLINGS

Chicago is home to seven medical schools, ninety-five hospitals, and fourteen national medical organizations, including the American Medical Association and the American Dental Association.

The first hospital in Illinois was Chicago's Mercy Hospital, built in 1863.

The first black civic institution in the city was Provident Hospital, built in 1891 by Daniel Hale Williams.

Bricks and Mortar

Grant Hospital, founded in 1883, was originally known as German Hospital.

From 1878 to 1886, a "Children's Sanitarium" was located in a pavilion erected on the North Avenue pier. Sick babies and their mothers were brought "from the hot and crowded city" in a steamboat chartered by the Floating Hospital Association to help them recuperate by the lake.

Chicago even honors the men and women in white with their very own Surgical Science Museum on Lake Shore Drive.

FROM DOCTORS' QUARTERS TO BUNNY HUTCH

The famous Playboy Mansion on North State Parkway, designed by James Gamble Rogers in 1903, was once the home and workshop of a physician. The house changed ownership several times before Playboy Enterprises purchased it in 1959 for $400,000—the property is worth more than $2 million today (that's a lot of carrots!). The mansion includes a ballroom, gourmet kitchen, underwater bar, and custom-made bowling alley and swimming pool, as well as a fireman's pole for unconventional access from one floor to the next.

The first permanent school building in the city was built by Ira Miltimore in 1845. It was ridiculed as "Miltimore's Folly" because of its hefty $7,500 construction price tag.

Railroad magnate and engineer George Pullman first gained notoriety in the city by having the Tremont House Hotel lifted twelve feet out of the mud without breaking one pane of glass or disturbing a single occupant.

Chicago's Coliseum was built stone by stone from the Civil War's Libby Prison transported to Chicago from Richmond, Virginia, by businessman Charles Gunther.

Chicago Convention and Tourism Bureau

WATER TOWER

William Boyington designed the only building to survive the Chicago Fire—the Water Tower, constructed of Joliet limestone, quarried in Illinois. The structure is now open to the public as a visitors' information center operated by the Chicago Convention and Tourism Bureau.

The Chicago Water Tower, constructed between 1867 and 1869, equalized water pressure throughout the entire city system through a 3-foot-wide, 138-foot-tall standpipe in its center.

A one-man band? No, a one-man bar. Chicago artist Frank Hesh built the Rathskeller on Superior Street using just one shovel. He also designed all the intricate designs carved onto the bar's wooden walls.

Did you ever wonder why homes erected before 1900 have their front door located on the second story? When the city built up the streets at the turn of the century to cover the newly installed sewer pipes, many Chicagoans discovered that their first floors had suddenly become basements and had to move their front entrance up a story.

6

By Any Other Name

"A rose by any other name," said the bard Shakespeare, "would smell as sweet." You'll come up smelling like a rose if you're privy to the meaning behind many of the following colloquial terms coined in Chicago.

Chicago businessman/benefactor Charles Gunther was known as "the Candy Man" for his invention of the caramel.

Chicago traces its name back to the Algonquin Indian word for the river, *checagou,* meaning "wild onion," "garlic," or "leek." For several years the Hyatt Regency Chicago celebrated the city's etymological history by naming its discotheque The Wild Onion. The city's name has withstood the test of time; the same cannot be said of the disco.

Early Chicago was known as "Slab City" because of the balloon houses constructed of boards that were built among the log cabins in the 1830s.

Chicago was once known as "the Garden City" due to the elaborate gardens and tree-lined yards surrounding the city's most magnificent homes.

The city motto in 1837 was "Urbs in Horta"—"a city in a garden."

The title of "Windy City" was bestowed on Chicago by *New York Sun* editor Charles Dana in 1893. He was tired of hearing "windy" Chicagoans boasting about the wonders of the world's Columbian Exposition.

Throughout its history, Chicago has also been known as "City in the Mud," "Pine Town," "Queen City of the Lakes," "Boss Town," "Porkopolis," and "Smoke and Steel."

A.K.A

In the late 1800s, the area of the city around Rush and Huron streets was known as "McCormickville." Twelve residences of the Cyrus McCormick family dominated the neighborhood, almost making it a city within itself.

Washington Square on Dearborn Street, located across from the Newberry Library, was once known as "Bedbug Square" because it was a favorite place for hoboes in the area.

Randolph Street, between Clark and State, was once referred to as "Hair-Trigger Block" due to the number of shootings that occurred there.

Because of constant mispronunciations, area residents proposed that Goethe Street be renamed Boxwood Place, Busse Place, or Nutwood Street, but the city council refused any such requests.

During the last two decades of the 1800s, South Michigan Avenue was dubbed "Millionaires' Row" due to the heavy concentration of wealthy captains of industry who built their homes there.

North Clark Street between the Chicago River and North Avenue was once billed by the press as "Honky-Tonk, USA." It was a well-known entertainment strip.

The corner of Oak and Orleans was known as "Death Corner." Many of Chicago's criminal element came out of

"Little Italy," also known as "Little Hell," bounded by Chicago Avenue, Wells Street, Division Street, and Larrabee Avenue.

TAKE ME OUT TO THE BALL GAME

"A Chicago decision," a baseball term meaning a shutout, takes its name from the Chicago White Stockings game in which they held their opponents without a run.

Chicago Bear Red Grange was nicknamed "the Wheaton Iceman" because of his summer job delivering ice to support himself at the University of Illinois.

The nickname "bleacher bums" to describe overenthusiastic fans originated in Chicago during the pennant playoffs at Wrigley Field in 1969.

Ernie Banks, who hit 512 home runs during a nineteen-year Chicago Cubs career, is known as "Mr. Sunshine."

The "suicide squad" was the nickname for the team of scientists led by Dr. Enrico Fermi in releasing the first controlled atomic nuclear chain reaction on December 2, 1942, at the University of Chicago.

"Tulip Tech" is the American Floral Art School, located on Wabash Avenue.

"Irish Power" was a term used in early Chicago to denote anything done by hand, because most of the Irish population were laborers.

Everyone in political office needs a "Chinaman," the Chicago term for a political sponsor.

"Field days," the American slang expression for a free-for-all, originated with Cyrus McCormick's day-long contests at the turn of the century that pitted his farm machines against those of his competitors.

The Fannie May candy stores were opened by real estate broker Archibald Teller in 1919 in Chicago. There was never a real Fannie May, it was only a name that Teller thought sounded like a candy maker.

Anti-German sentiment in Chicago during World War I caused the renaming of the Germania Club to the Chicago Lincoln Club, the Hotel Bismark to the Hotel Randolph, and the Hotel Kaiserhof to the Hotel Atlantic.

Notorious ward alderman "Bathhouse" John Coughlin got his nickname from his early job as the fellow who gave the rubdowns in a Turkish bath.

HIGH SOCIETY

"Silk Stockings" was the name given to the wealthy residents of the fashionable eastern side of the Second Ward, directly opposite the western "Levee" District, a high vice and crime district (named after the levee areas along the Mississippi delta).

The Grasshoppers was an elegant social club of residents along Ashland Avenue during the 1800s, taking its name from the fact that the ladies' skirts were covered with grasshoppers as they passed through the fields to each others' homes.

7

Playtime

Chicago is often called the City That Works, but its citizens also love to party. They hosted two major world's fairs, and in recent years the city has been sponsoring civic festivals year-round.

Not all the entertainment and diversions that Chicagoans partake of have been legit, but even the turn-of-the-century bordellos, bright lights, and clandestine gambling casinos and speakeasys add to the glamorous image of how Chicagoans relax and refresh the spirit.

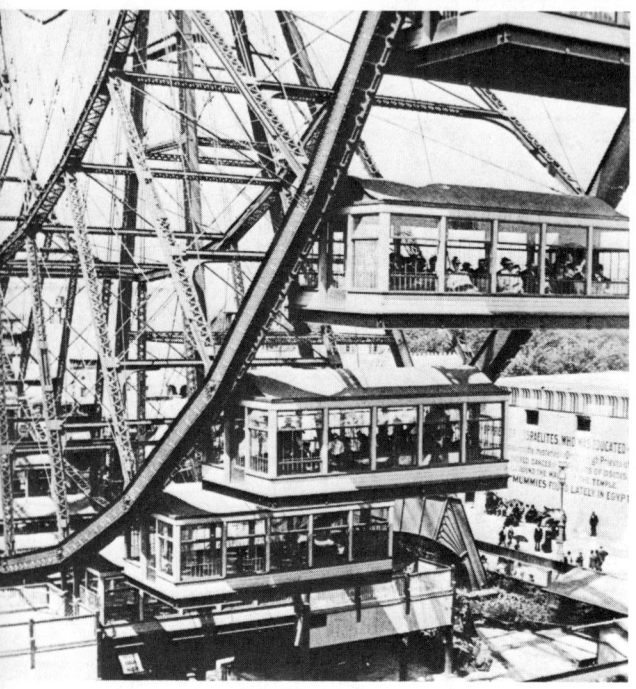
Chicago Historical Society

Chicago Convention and Tourism Bureau

THE WORLD'S COLUMBIAN EXPOSITION

The Ferris wheel made its debut in Chicago in 1893. At the invitation of Daniel Burnham to create an attraction for the World's Columbian Exposition that would "rival the Eiffel Tower," George W. G. Ferris designed a giant wheel that stood 250 feet above the ground and had thirty-six cars holding forty people.

Still in existence today and dating from the exposition are the Museum of Science and Industry, La Rabida Children's Hospital, Jackson and Washington parks, and the Midway Plaisance.

The fair attracted 27 million visitors, almost one-half the total population in the United States at the time.

The Exposition took three years to build, and more than $5 million in funds was needed to construct the Jackson Park lakefront site.

NAUGHTY BUT NICE

For more than twenty years, Carrie Watson helped put a smile on the faces of Chicago politicians and businessmen. Her notorious cathouse at 441 South Clark Street came complete with a billiard room and bowling alley for added diversion.

The patrons in Watson's bordello were often given iced bottles of champagne to use as pins in the bowling alley.

City visitors looking for a good time at the turn of the century sought out the "Levee" District, State and Wabash between Adams and Twelfth streets. This was a popular site for illegal pursuits of all sorts, named after the levee areas along the Mississippi River in Memphis and New Orleans, where vice was rampant.

A popular gambling saloon and hangout for the rogues of the late nineteeth century was The Store, owned by Michael Cassius "King Mike" McDonald at Clark and Monroe streets.

In February of 1870, Chicagoans got an eyeful when Lydia "Black Crook" Thompson and her British Blondes were the first burlesque troupe to perform in the city.

On February 1, 1900, sisters Ada and Minna Everleigh opened the Everleigh Club at 2131-2133 South Dearborn. It was tabbed "the most elegant and costly brothel in the world"—prices for a young lady's affections started at fifty dollars. The club was closed down under the orders of Mayor Carter Harrison II on October 24, 1911.

DID YOU KNOW . . .

The city's 574 parks contain 7,300 acres.

Chicago has twenty-nine miles of lake frontage and fifteen miles of public beach.

Looking for some unusual entertainment? Try one of the following:

> magician bartenders at the New York Lounge on North Lincoln Avenue
> male strippers at the One, Two, Three Club on Diversey
> a medieval banquet at the King's Manor on Lawrence Avenue
> the Men's $1.98 Leg Contest at Sally's Stage on North Western Avenue
> turtle races at the Ship's Rail Bar, Dolton Lounge, at 154th Street
> women's mud wrestling at Kukla's Restaurant and Lounge on South Cicero

Sure beats the pink elephants that hang out at your neighborhood bar!

ENTERTAINMENT FIRSTS

The city got its first taste of culture when its first opera was presented in John B. Rice's theater in 1850—*La Sonnambula*. An extended engagement was cut short, however, when fire destroyed the theater on opening night.

The first of Chicago's elegant little hotels was the Lake House located at Rush and North Water streets. Guests were treated to such amenities as napkins, toothpicks, and printed menus in the dining room, which also boasted the talents of an honest-to-goodness French chef.

The first main stage attraction to appear at the first ChicagoFest in 1978 was the Atlanta Rhythm Section and Eddie Money.

Chicago's first nightclub, built in 1898, was the Friar's Inn.

Hugh Hefner began the revolution for freedom of sexual expression by starting *Playboy* at 6052 South Harper Street in 1953. The first issue sold for fifty cents and featured for "the first time in any magazine—full color—the famous Marilyn Monroe nude."

SEE YOU AT THE FAIR

The area used to house the Century of Progress Exposition in 1933 eventually became the city's Burnham Park.

Chicago Convention and Tourism Bureau

Chicago Historical Society

One of the major attractions of the world's fair of 1933 was fan dancer Sally Rand, who once commented that once she began taking off her clothes, she never again stood in the unemployment line.

FESTIVALS

Winter blizzards may have ended the political career of Mayor Michael Bilandic, but he was the man responsible for giving the city its most successful summer festival—ChicagoFest.

"Saturday Night Live" Blues Brothers John Belushi and Dan Ackroyd created quite a stir when they helped ChicagoFest vendor Sam Sianis cook hamburgers at his Billy Goat festival stand in 1979. OK, who ordered the cheez-borger, cheez-borger?

One of Chicago's oldest neighborhood parades—the Bud Billiken Day parade—takes its name from the Oriental god of happiness, the Billiken, and the nickname of the editor of the parade's sponsor, the *Defender,* Lucius "Bud" Harper. The annual event started in 1929 to honor poor newsboys on the city's South Side.

FOR THOSE WHO THINK SHORT

The Midget Club is located at 4016 West Sixty-third Street; the owners are midgets, and everything in the club is low to the ground.

BARGAIN HUNTING

The largest outdoor flea market in Chicago is Maxwell Street, located 1300 South on Halsted. It's a great place for early Sunday morning browsing through everything from funk to junk.

THE HORSEY SET

Chicago once rivaled the thoroughbred activity of the Blue Grass State with its own American Derby Races. Between 1884 and 1904, the horsey set in town could be found at the Washington Park Race Track at Sixty-first and Cottage Grove.

Veloz and Yolanda were the opening night's entertainment when the Empire Room in the Palmer House premiered as a supper club in 1933. They proved so popular they were held over for thirty-seven weeks.

ENJOY THE RIDE

The world's largest amusement park was once located in Chicago at 3300 North Western Avenue. Riverview originally opened in 1904 as the German Sharpshooter Park, an actual hunting preserve.

8

All the News That's Fit to Print

Extra! Extra! Read all about the fourth estate in Chicago, the newsmakers and exposé breakers who have all practiced their craft in a town that still spawns award-winning journalism.

JOURNALISM FIRSTS

The first official newspaper in town premiered on November 26, 1833, with the publication of John Calhoun's *Chicago Democrat*. The paper, a six-column weekly edited and published by Calhoun, was absorbed by the *Chicago Tribune* in 1861.

The first issue of the *Chicago Tribune* came off the presses on June 10, 1847, printed from a third-floor room at LaSalle and Lake streets.

Chicago's first tabloid paper was *The Times*, founded in 1929 by Samuel Emory Thomason.

Chicago Volksfreund, founded in 1845, was Chicago's first German newspaper.

Chicago's first Sunday newspaper, *Der Westen*, went on sale in 1854.

The first newspaper column in the country started in the *Chicago Tribune* with Bert Taylor's "A Line-O-Type or Two."

The city's first black newspaper, *The Conservator*, was founded in 1878 by Ferdinand L. Barnett.

OOPS

The front page of the November 3, 1948, *Chicago Tribune* carried the infamous "Dewey Defeats Truman" headline. This postelection issue had been put to bed before the polls in the East had reported their results. The paper's chief competitor committed a similar gaffe during the Republican National Convention of 1980, when a *Sun-Times* headline blared "It's Reagan and Ford," when, in fact, George Bush—not Gerald Ford—had been nominated for the vice-presidency.

THE BRIGHT ONE

The *Chicago Sun*, parent paper of today's *Sun-Times*, was founded by Marshall Field III, grandson of the department store magnate, in 1941.

The Chicago *Sun-Times* was born in 1948, a merger of two newspapers, the *Sun* and the *Times*.

The most widely syndicated newspaper column in the world originates in the Chicago *Sun-Times*—"Ann Landers," written by Eppie Lederer and carried by more than one thousand newspapers.

When Melville Stone premiered the *Chicago Daily News* on Christmas Day of 1875, the paper sold for a penny and refused to sully its pages with commercial advertising.

The *Inter-Ocean* newspaper sponsored a contest in 1891 to design a symbol of Chicago's character. The "I Will" figure submitted by artist Charles Holloway won first honors.

One of the smallest daily newspapers ever produced was printed in Chicago. The *Day Book* could neatly fit into a man's breast pocket even without folding it.

9

Says Who?

Talk is not only cheap, it is often surprisingly durable. We've all said some things that have lasted a bit *too* long and have come back to us; the following phrases have even lasted beyond their speakers.

Out of the mouths of these Chicagoans have come words of wisdom, puns, and platitudes. So the next time you hear any of these expressions, you'll know they were spoken first in Chicago.

First impressions aren't necessarily the right ones. Legend has it that an old Shawnee town banker refused a loan to Chicago in the 1870s, snidely declaring, "It will never amount to anything!" A lot he knew.

The mottoes of Marshall Field's department store are, "Give the lady what she wants," and "The customer is always right."

"Nobody's on the legit" and "Ya keep ya nose clean, ya understand?" were favorite expressions of gangster Al Capone, Chicago's most legendary hood.

Though often attributed to circus showman P. T. Barnum, the phrase "There's a sucker born every minute" was actually coined by Chicago's King of the Gamblers, Mike McDonald.

Mayor William Emmett Dever (1923–1927) had as his motto, "Chicago always is entitled to first place." His administration was responsible for 190 miles of street paving, the completion of double-decker Wacker Drive, and the straightening of the Chicago River.

Charles Tyson Yerkes, shrewd operator of the Loop elevated lines in the early twentieth century, had as his business motto, "Buy old junk and fix it up a little and unload it on others before it wears out."

Wrigley Field announcer Pat Pieper popularized the phrase "play ball."

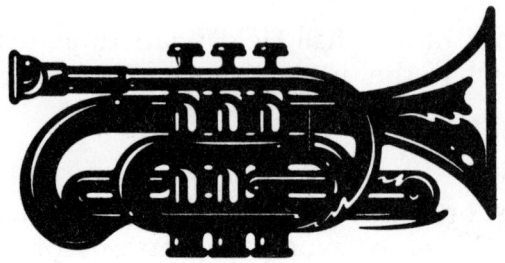

10

All That Jazz

If it's true that music has charms to soothe the savage breast, then Chicagoans have every reason to be serenely content. In the 1920s, Chicago gave "jazz" to music lovers throughout the world. And with a song in its heart, this love affair with good music continues today, culminating in the biggest music festival in the country—ChicagoFest—held annually on Navy Pier at the lakefront.

IMMORTALIZED IN SONG

The words and the music for "Chicago (That Toddling Town)" were written in 1922 by Fred Fisher. Popular in the 1920s in vaudeville acts, the song was used as the background music for *Little Giant,* starring Edward G. Robinson in 1933, and *Beyond the Forest,* with Bette Davis in 1949. An RCA recording of it by Tommy Dorsey and his orchestra was a 1930s bestseller.

"Old Blue Eyes" himself, Frank Sinatra, introduced the song "My Kind of Town (Chicago Is)" in the 1964 Warner Brothers musical *Robin and the Seven Hoods.* With words by Sammy Cahn and music by Jimmy Van Heusen, the song was voted the best motion picture song of 1964 by the All-American Press Association.

A domestic quarrel witnessed in Chicago by songwriter Charles Harris in 1892 became the inspiration for the popular song "After the Ball." The song was performed by John Philip Sousa at the 1893 World's Fair and from then on was always a part of Sousa's program or used as an encore.

Songstress Sophie Tucker introduced the song "Some of These Days" at the White City Park in Chicago in 1910; the song went on to become her theme song.

"Ain't She Sweet?" was introduced to the public at the Oriental Theatre in Chicago in 1927 by Paul Ash and his orchestra and became an instant hit.

MUSICAL FIRSTS

Chicago's first hotelier, Mark Beaubien, was well known for his fiddle playing. Beaubien, who had twenty-three children by three wives, obviously didn't spend all his spare time making music.

Ferdinand Wythe Peck is credited with bringing the first opera to Chicago.

In 1891, Theodore Thomas became the first conductor of the Chicago Symphony Orchestra.

NOTEWORTHY FACTS

Chicagoan George Root wrote the "Battle Cry of Freedom," a popular song during America's Civil War.

The term *jazz* was coined in Chicago in 1914. The city's native musicians include band leader Benny Goodman and drummer Gene Krupa.

Chicago was once a leading manufacturer of musical instruments. In the mid-nineteenth century, Julius Bauer's factory on Clark Street produced melodeons, accordions, concertinas, violins, flutes, guitars, drums, tambourines, banjos, and German silver and brass band instruments.

11

Street Signs

Streets are one of the many advantages of city life that we tend to take for granted. It's difficult to imagine that Chicago's streets didn't exist from day one, complete with potholes.

The city's highways and byways didn't just materialize overnight. They evolved from cow paths and muddy covered wagon trails into an orderly system of nicely paved thoroughfares on which Chicagoans park their cars, hold their parades, and travel to and from their daily destinations.

Street Signs 59

STREET NAMES

Many of the streets in Chicago's downtown business district were named by its first surveyor, James Thompson. Thompson named the following thoroughfares: Washington, Randolph, Carroll, Kinzie, Dearborn, Clark, Clinton, and Jefferson.

STREET NUMBERS

The street-numbering scheme was devised by city ordinance in 1908. State Street was established as the baseline running north and south. Madison Street as the baseline running east and west. One hundred numbers are assigned to each one-eighth mile: even numbers for buildings on the north and west sides, and odd numbers for buildings on the south and east sides.

NO BOTTOM HERE

Chicago streets during most of the nineteenth century were unpaved and in rainy weather became seas of mud. It was a common sight to see poles stuck in deep mud holes with a sign noting, "No bottom here—the shortest road to China." A popular tall tale of the day involved travelers seeing a man up to his neck in mud who reassured onlookers that he was standing on his horse.

Even paved, Chicago wasn't always a city of concrete. In 1871, the majority of Chicago's streets were wood paved by a process known as the "Nicholson pavement." Planks were swabbed with tar, and then topped with wooden blocks, and sealed with tar and pebbles.

THAT GREAT STREET

State Street wasn't always Chicago's "Great Street." The main business thoroughfare in the mid-nineteenth century was Lake Street where land sold for two thousand dollars a front foot compared with two hundred dollars on State Street, considered to be "narrow, shoddy, and unpromising."

State Street takes its name from being an old state road. It was widened in 1867 by twenty-seven feet, greatly helping it become "that great street" of shopping and business.

THE LOOP

Wabash Avenue, Lake Street, Wells Street, and Van Buren Street determine the boundaries of the Loop and are the streets running below the elevated trains.

DID YOU KNOW THAT . . .

The center of the city is located at 3700 South Honore.

The first paved street in the city was on South Wells between South Water and Lake Street, laid by civil engineer Samuel S. Greeley.

A block-long Chicago street is also a Chicago landmark—Alta Vista Terrace, running for one block north and south from 1050 West Grace Street.

Western Avenue, stretching for 24.5 miles, is the longest continuous street within city limits in the world.

Lake Street received its name because it ran into Lake Michigan.

Hubbard Trail, carved out by fur trader Gordon "Swift Walker" Hubbard, eventually became the State Road in 1834, running from Vincennes, Indiana, to Chicago, and eventually becoming the present-day State Street.

The Midway Plaisance, the driveway connecting Jackson and Washington parks and the site of the 1893 world's fair, takes its name from its location between the two parks and the French word *plaisance* meaning a "place of pleasure."

Chicago Historical Society, photo by Walter E. Angier, C.E.

Hey, New York! Chicago once had its own Fifth Avenue. Wells Street was renamed Fifth Avenue in 1870, but the name was changed back to Wells Street in 1918.

The Board of Trade Court is a private street, running 324 south, east and west 140 to 160.

North Michigan Avenue was originally labeled Pine Street as far north as Oak Street.

CONDO KING

Real estate mogul Arthur Rubloff is credited with creating the term "Magnificent Mile" to describe the ritzy strip of shops, hotels, and restaurants along North Michigan Avenue.

Chicago has 3,679 miles of street, the busiest stretch being the Dan Ryan Expressway at Fifty-ninth Street. Every day, 250,000 vehicles pass by this point.

WHATEVER BECAME OF . . .

Twelfth Street became Roosevelt Road after the death of Teddy Roosevelt.

Tyler Street was renamed Congress Street to honor the U.S. Senate and was later extended to the Eisenhower Expressway.

Twenty-second Street became Cermak Road to honor assassinated mayor Anton Cermak.

Street Signs 63

The Southwest Expressway, opened in 1964, was renamed the Adlai E. Stevenson Expressway in 1965 to honor the former governor of Illinois.

The Northwest Expressway, opened in 1960 to connect the Eisenhower Expressway with O'Hare International Airport, was renamed the John F. Kennedy Expressway.

The Congress Street superhighway was renamed the Dwight D. Eisenhower Expressway in 1964 by action of the Chicago City Council.

Montrose Boulevard was originally called Sulzer Road after Konrad Sulzer, one of the city's first brewmasters.

Belmont Avenue was once known as Chase Avenue after Blanchard Chase, whose house stood where the street ended. It was renamed after Belmont, Missouri, where Ulysses S. Grant first commanded Union troops during the Civil War.

Washington Street was originally known as Church Street, because the First and Second Presbyterian, Methodist, Baptist, Unitarian, and Universalist churches were all located along this street.

Broadway was once known as Evanston Avenue, Plank Road, Clarendon Avenue, Lake Shore Avenue, and Dummy Road.

Ashland Avenue was once known as Reuben Street, but local residents demanded a name change when the derogatory expression "Hey, Rube!" came into fashion. The name Ashland comes from the country home of Kentuckian Henry Clay.

Chestnut Street was once called Hinsdale Street.

Crawford Avenue, named for early pioneer Peter Crawford, was later changed to Pulaski Road.

Grand Avenue was originally called Indiana Avenue.

BOUNDARIES AND NEIGHBORHOODS

Ravenswood got its name from local German inhabitants who heard ravens in the nearby forests.

North Avenue was the northernmost city boundary until 1862.

Division Street divided Chicago proper from its northern neighborhoods.

Western Avenue was the westernmost boundary of the city until 1853.

Streeterville, the area in the city's Near North Side bounded by the Chicago River, East Lake Shore Drive, Lake Michigan, and Michigan Avenue, was founded and named by Captain George Wellington Streeter, who ran his scow aground there and declared his own city.

Cottage Grove Avenue took its name from the lone cabin that stood there in the early nineteenth century.

STREETS NAMED IN HONOR OF . . .

Fulton Street was named for steamboat inventor Robert Fulton.

Clinton Street honors DeWitt Clinton, politician responsible for the construction of the Erie Canal.

LaSalle Street was named for Robert Cavelier, sieur de La Salle, who explored the region in the seventeenth century.

Clark Street, once spelled Clarke, was named for explorer George Rogers Clark.

Franklin Street takes it name from the American statesman and inventor Benjamin Franklin.

Carroll Street was named for Declaration of Independence signer Charles Carroll.

Randolph Street honors U.S. patriot John Randolph of Virginia.

Adams, Madison, Monroe, Jackson, Van Buren, Harrison, Tyler, Polk, Taylor, and Fillmore were named after U.S. presidents.

Wells Street was named for Captain William Wells, killed during the Fort Dearborn massacre.

Ogden Avenue was named for Chicago's first mayor, William B. Ogden.

Wentworth Avenue honors Mayor "Long John" Wentworth.

Canal Street commemorated the construction of the Illinois and Michigan Canal.

HONORING . . .

Halsted Street—Philadelphia banker William Halsted
Irving Park Road—writer Washington Irving
Burnham Avenue—architect and city planner Daniel Burnham
Clybourn Avenue—Chicago's first constable, Archibald Clybourn
Addison Street—English physician Thomas Addison
Balbo Drive—Gen. Italo Balbo
Lawrence Avenue—Bradford Lawrence
Fullerton Avenue—Chicago's first clerk of town trustees, Alexander Fullerton
Wilson Avenue—University of Chicago benefactor John P. Wilson
Peterson Avenue—parks system benefactor Peter Samuel Peterson
Kedzie Avenue—real estate developer John Hume Kedzie

Cornell Avenue and Cornell Drive—Hyde Park founder Paul Cornell
Archer Avenue—Illinois and Michigan Canal commissioner Col. William Archer
Oakley Avenue—Illinois and Michigan Canal commissioner Charles Oakley
Lincoln Avenue—President Abraham Lincoln
Todd Street—Mary Todd Lincoln
Sheridan Road—Union Army Gen. Philip Sheridan
Pershing Road—World War I Gen. John Pershing
Rush Street, also known as "That Street of Dreams"— Declaration of Independence signer Dr. Benjamin Rush
Maxwell Street—Fort Dearborn surgeon Philip Maxwell
Loomis Boulevard—Board of Trade organizer Horatio Loomis
Wabash Avenue—Wapashaw, chief of the Dakota tribe
Damen Avenue—Rev. Father Arnold Damen, founder of the Jesuit missions in the West and Holy Family Parish
Carmen Street—Carmen, the lead character in Bizet's opera of the same name.

ETC.

Monitor, Merrimac, and Kearsarge streets are named for Civil War naval ships.

Dearborn Street takes its name from the fifth U.S. secretary of state, General Henry Dearborn.

Beaubien Court, running north and south parallel to the Prudential Building, is named in honor of the city's first innkeeper, Mark Beaubien.

Diversey Street takes its name from Michael Diversey, operator of Chicago's first brewery.

Wacker Drive, considered by some to be the Park Avenue of Chicago, was named after civic benefactor and brewmaster Charles Wacker.

Civil War Union generals Mead, Grant, Hooker, Logan, Banks, McClellan, and Burnside all have streets named after them in Chicago.

The Dan Ryan Expressway, opened in 1962, was named for the president of the Cook County Board of Commissioners.

Quincy Street is named for John Quincy Adams, who lost the presidential election to Andrew Jackson.

Hermitage, Ashland, Kenmore, and Monticello avenues are all named after historic estates: Andrew Jackson's home in Tennessee, Henry Clay's home in Kentucky, Col. Lewis Fielding's home in Virginia, and Thomas Jefferson's estate in Virginia.

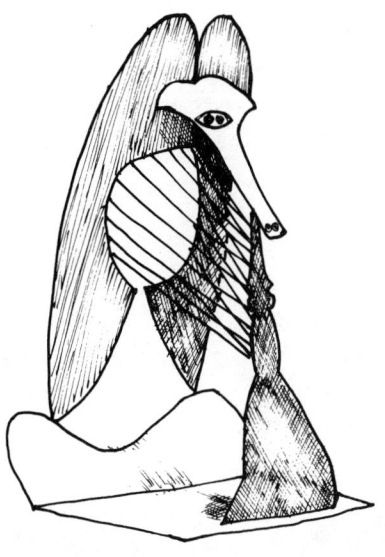

12

We Got Class

The Midwest is by no means the cultural desert that other parts of the country make it out to be. In reality, the benefaction of many of Chicago's well-to-do has ensured a wealth of cultural heritage for the city, enjoyed by resident and visitor alike.

In addition to hosting some of the finest museums found anywhere in the world, Chicago shows off its interest in the fine arts with a collection of sidewalk sculpture unmatched by any other major U.S. city today.

SCULPTURES

America's boom in urban sidewalk sculpture began in downtown Chicago, which boasts works by such artistic notables as Pablo Picasso, Marc Chagall, Alexander Calder, and Harry Bertoia.

You may never guess it, but the Picasso sculpture at the Daley Civic Center Plaza, Randolph and Dearborn streets, represents "the head of a woman," according to the artist. Its message is, "A woman, like a city, is a two-faced thing."

Chicago Convention and Tourism Bureau

Among the sculptures in Chicago's Lincoln Park area is an honest-to-goodness Indian totem pole at Addison and Lake Shore Drive. It was brought to Chicago in 1929 from the Queen Charlotte Islands of British Columbia.

A monument to that great American pastime, baseball, stands in front of the U.S. Social Security Administration Building at 600 West Madison—Claes Oldenburg's eighty-foot-tall *Batcolumn* sculpture. Sculptor Oldenburg originally wanted to build a giant fireplug painted bright red for the Social Security Building, but he settled instead for the world's biggest baseball bat.

Four historical figures have multiple sculptures honoring them in Chicago parks: Christopher Columbus has two, George Washington has three, Abraham Lincoln has four, and Alexander Hamilton has two.

When Alexander Calder's *Flamingo* sculpture was unveiled on Dearborn Street in the Federal Center in 1973, he rode to the ceremony in style, atop a circus wagon at the head of a full-fledged circus parade.

The courtyard in front of the Standard Oil Building boasts the only Chicago sculpture that "talks;" Harry Bertoia's *Sounding Sculpture* of metal rods.

MUSEUMS

Chicago's leading tourism attraction, drawing some 4 million visitors annually, was founded by Julius Rosenwald in 1933—the Museum of Science and Industry.

Chicago Convention and Tourism Bureau

The Adler Planetarium, opened to the public in 1930, was made possible by a $1 million gift from Sears, Roebuck executive Max Adler.

Chicago Convention and Tourism Bureau

John Graves Shedd, one-time president and chairman of the board of Marshall Field & Company, presented the Shedd Aquarium as a "gift to the people of Chicago" in 1929.

Department store mogul Marshall Field's donation of $1 million started the Field Museum of Natural History in 1893. Over the next fifty years, the Field family donated an additional $20 million to ensure the growth of the museum. The Field Museum's collections are so extensive that less than one-half of 1 percent of all its specimens and artifacts are on display in the museum at any one time, the remainder being kept in storage.

Chicago Convention and Tourism Bureau

BIG SPENDERS

Lumber magnate Benjamin Ferguson donated the $1 million Ferguson Fund in 1905, earmarked for sculptures in the parks and along the boulevards to "commemorate worthy men or women of America or important events of American history." A walk through any of Chicago's 574 parks shows the results of Ferguson's generosity.

Chicago Convention and Tourism Bureau

Not to be outdone by a lumber magnate, Kate Sturges Buckingham donated $750,000 to the city in 1927 for construction of the Buckingham Fountain as a memorial to her brother Clarence.

Some gifts are better than others. Although three foundations offered to underwrite the cost of a sculpture for the Daley Civic Center Plaza—the Woods Charitable Fund, Inc.; the Chauncey and Marion Deering McCormick Foundation; and the Field Foundation of Illinois—artist Pablo Picasso contributed his sculpture as a "gift to the people of Chicago."

Chicago's art works are weighty matters in more ways than one:

Calder's *Flamingo* at the Federal Center weighs fifty tons.

The *Universe* mobile in the lobby of Sears Tower weighs eight tons.

The Picasso sculpture in the Daley Civic Center Plaza tips the scales at 162 tons.

———•—•———

Charley Hutchinson, one of the founders of the Academy of Fine Arts, spearheaded the drive to build the Art Institute in 1882.

From fine tuning to fine arts—the Fine Arts Building at 410 South Michigan Avenue was originally used by the Studebaker brothers as a sales center for carriages and wagons.

When the French government loaned *Whistler's Mother* to the Art Institute in 1933 for the world's fair, it arrived via armored truck and was insured for $1 million.

The *Wall of Respect* at Forty-third and Langley was the first of more than 130 Chicago murals painted in neighborhoods throughout the city beginning in 1967.

The main entrance to Chicago's City Hall features four granite sculptured panels created by artist John Flanagan to honor four features of city government: playgrounds, public schools, parks, and the water supply system.

Artist Les Levine immortalized the Wrigley chewing gum empire by creating a series of solid gold chewing gum sculptures from a six-pack of Wrigley's Doublemint gum he chewed for the project.

13

Catastrophes

Without a doubt, the worst tragedy to befall Chicago was the Great Fire of 1871. But as much as it was a time of trial and tempest, it grew to become a time of triumph as the city rebuilt, expanded, and flourished.

In every disaster that has struck the city or its citizens since that time, the determination and "I Will" spirit of the people have valiantly come through.

THE CHICAGO FIRE

The Chicago Fire of 1871 destroyed a mere 3.2 square miles of the city's total 35 square miles. This area, however, comprised the entire central business district.

The location of the start of the fire has been pinpointed to DeKoven Street between Clinton and Jefferson.

Kate O'Leary owned the cow with a twitchy foot that allegedly tipped over the lantern that started the blaze. Ironically, the Chicago Fire Academy now occupies the site of the fire's origin.

It figures. The first business to rebuild after the Great Fire was a real estate office. Plucky businessman W. D. Kerfoot tacked up the following sign on his office at 59 Union Park Place (Washington and LaSalle), rolled up his sleeves, and went to work: "All gone but wife, children, and energy."

While other buildings surrounding it burned to the ground, the 119-year-old Tap Root Pub on West Willow managed to survive the fire without damage.

THE HOUSE SAVED BY CIDER

Policeman Richard Bellinger's cottage on Hudson Avenue was saved from destruction during the Great Fire when the quick-thinking Bellinger doused the flames with apple cider when his water supply was gone.

MAN OVERBOARD!

The worst Chicago tragedy on Lake Michigan was the overturning of the *Eastland* at the Clark Street dock in 1915—eight hundred attendees of a General Electric company outing drowned.

Chicagoans lost a yearly holiday tradition when the *Rouse Simmons,* known as "the Christmas Tree Ship," sank off Two Rivers Point, Wisconsin, in 1912. It was so called because it carried balsam and spruce trees into the Clark Street dock in Chicago for the holidays.

Three ships lie beneath Lake Michigan's waters off Chicago's shoreline: the *Lady Elgin,* a luxury passenger steamboat that sank in 1860, drowning 297 off Winnetka; the *Flora Hill,* a steamer that sank in 1912, one-half mile off Navy Pier with a cargo of carbide headlamps for antique Cadillacs; and the SS *Iowa,* a steamer crushed by ice in 1915, lying one and a half miles off Navy Pier.

MORE TRAGEDY

The worst tragedy in Chicago's theatrical history occurred on December 30, 1903, when the Iroquois Theatre caught fire during a performance by Eddie Foy. Six hundred lives were lost.

The two world's fairs held in Chicago were overshadowed by tragedy: Mayor Carter H. Harrison I was assassinated in 1893, and Mayor Anton Cermak was assassinated in 1933 prior to the opening of the Century of Progress Exposition.

14

Star Gazing

Psst. Isn't that Frank Sinatra in the Pump Room's Booth One?

Chicago is no slouch when it comes to celebrities—those who trace their roots here, those who practiced their craft and achieved fame here, and those who frequent our trendy eateries and night spots, causing heads to turn and necks to crane, asking, "Isn't that . . .?"

80 THE CHICAGO TRIVIA BOOK

GOSSIP MILL GRIST

Columnist Irv Kupcinet began reporting on this town's coosome twosomes and other celebrity notables in "Kup's Column" in the 1943 *Sun-Times,* making Kup himself a celebrity after almost four decades of reporting.

Lettuce Entertain You Enterprises

ROLLING OUT THE RED CARPET FOR ROYALTY

One royal visitor to Chicago set a record for luggage that has gone unmatched by celebrity or conventioneer since. Prince Henry of Prussia checked into the Auditorium Hotel at Michigan and Congress in 1902 with 183 pieces. We hope the bellboy got a big tip!

Prince Henry was a true romantic. The tradition of drinking champagne from a lady's shoe allegedly started at Chicago's Everleigh Club, when the prince drank some bubbly out of a dancing girl's slipper that had conveniently fallen into his lap.

The first royal visitor to Chicago was King Edward VII, then Prince of Wales, in 1860.

Queen Marie of Romania was the first woman to break the ban on women's smoking at the prestigious all-male Union League Club of Chicago in 1926. Assistant maître d' Albert Pein had to be restrained from presenting her with a white card that formally noted, "Please! Ladies are not allowed to smoke."

THE PUMP ROOM

Actress Gertrude Lawrence was the first celebrity to grace the Pump Room's Booth One. She came to Chicago to star in *Susan & God* nine days after the posh restaurant opened on October 1, 1938, and made the first booth inside the ritzy establishment her second home when she was not in her hotel room or at the theater.

Lettuce Entertain You Enterprises

The Pump Room takes its name from the health resort discovered during the heyday of the Roman Empire and located in Bath, England. It was named for the hot water drinks it pumped to cure a variety of its patrons' ills.

Celebrities wishing to steer clear of the limelight of the Pump Room's Booth One can have a secretive tête-à-tête in the Green Booth, a velvet banquette hidden away in the back corner of the room.

ART'S PART

Some of the greatest names in American art—10 percent of the names listed in the *Who's Who in American Art*—graduated from the Chicago School of the Art Institute, including Halston, Claes Oldenberg, Georgia O'Keeffe, and Robert Indiana.

CELEBRITY CIRCLES

Chicago's Lake Shore Drive social circle boasts a descendant of Buffalo Bill Cody—socialite Abra Prentice Anderson, also the great-granddaughter of tycoon John D. Rockefeller.

In an effort to cater to its posh celebrity clientele, Chicago Limousine Service outfitted its fleet with a special white stretch limousine for singer Barry Manilow, only to discover that when the crooner arrived in town, he had changed his mind and preferred the traditional black.

The original "Ann Landers" advice columnist was Ruth Crowley, who wrote an "Ask Ann Landers" column for the Chicago *Sun-Times* until her death in 1955.

Author Ernest Hemingway was a one-time Chicago resident; during the summer of 1920, he lived at 100 East Chicago Avenue and met his first wife, Hadley Richardson, there.

Channel 2 award-winning news anchor Walter "Skippy" Jacobson was once a Chicago Cubs batboy.

Comedian Joe E. Brown and President Ronald "Dutch" Reagan were among those who announced Chicago baseball games over the radio.

CLOTHES HORSE

Social butterflies who want their wardrobes preserved for posterity can donate them to the Chicago Historical Society, but only if the garment has been made in Chicago, worn by a Chicagoan, or worn to a special event in Chicago.

Fashion designer Halston got his start in the business by designing hats at the Ambassador East Hotel beauty salon.

HOTEL HOPPING

"Piano Man" Billy Joel registers as "Mr. Allie Gorie" whenever he checks into the Westin Hotel.

Coosome twosomes who enjoyed honeymoon bliss at the Ambassador East Hotel included Nicky Hilton and Elizabeth Taylor, and Frank Sinatra and Barbara Marx.

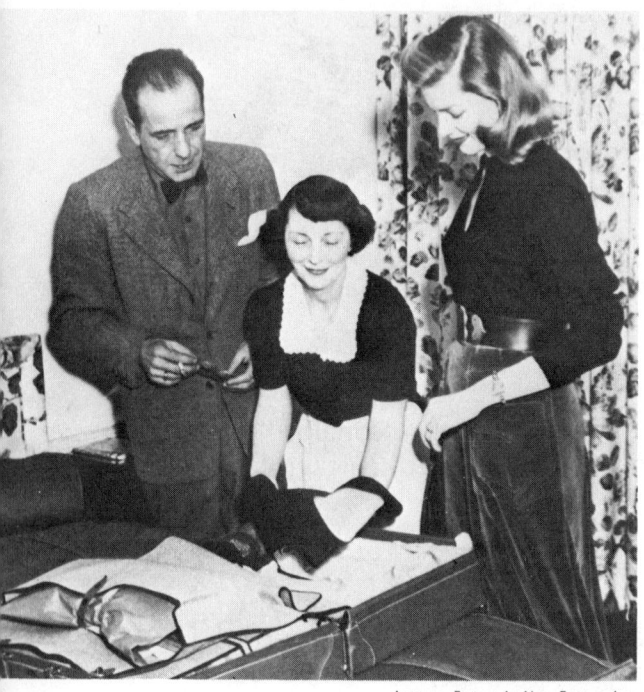

Lettuce Entertain You Enterprises

Newlyweds Lauren Bacall and tough guy movie star Humphrey Bogart also honeymooned at the Ambassador East Hotel, where they nuzzled as they nibbled on wedding cake in the Pump Room's Booth One.

Twelve presidents of the United States have slept in the Presidential Suite of the Blackstone Hotel. The baby grand piano in the parlor was a favorite of Harry S. Truman.

A native of Illinois and fortieth president of the United States, Ronald Reagan frequents the Drake Hotel barber shop whenever he needs a shave and a haircut while visiting the Windy City.

The following celebrities were born in Chicago:

Morey Amsterdam (1912)
Ralph Bellamy (1904)

Edgar Bergen (1903)
Shelley Berman (1924)

Star Gazing 85

Tom Bosley (1927)
Gene Cernan (1934)
John Chancellor (1927)
Robert Conrad (1937)
Walt Disney (1901)
Mike Douglas (1925)
Bob Fosse (1927)
Mitzi Gaynor (1931)
George Gobel (1920)
Benny Goodman (1909)
Virginia Graham (1912)
Dolores Gray (1930)
Hugh Hefner (1926)
Skip Homeier (1930)
Richard Kiley (1922)
Dorothy Kilgallen (1913)
Gene Krupa (1909)
Frankie Laine (1913)
Jack E. Leonard (1911)
Ramsey Lewis (1935)
Norman Luboff (1917)

Jock Mahoney (1919)
Karl Malden (1914)
Barbara McNair (1937)
Vincente Minnelli (1913)
Bob Newhart (1929)
Kim Novak (1933)
Donald O'Connor (1925)
William Paley (1901)
Jason Robards, Jr. (1922)
Robert Ryan (1913)
Allan Sherman (1924)
Gloria Swanson (1899)
June Taylor (1918)
Burr Tillstrom (1917)
Mel Tormé (1925)
Irving Wallace (1916)
Hal B. Wallis (1899)
Sam Wanamaker (1919)
Robert Young (1907)
Florenz Ziegfeld (1869)

Celebrities who trace their theatrical beginnings to Chicago include:

Steve Allen
Jim Belushi
John Belushi
Jack Benny
Phil Foster
Charlton Heston
Rock Hudson
Cloris Leachman
Paul Lynde

Ann-Margret
Elaine May
Mike Nichols
Tyrone Power
Danny Thomas
Mike Todd
Mike Wallace
Orson Welles

Chicago went Hollywood when the following places were among the locations used in the filming of:

My Bodyguard: The Ambassador East Hotel was home to general manager Martin Mull and his wacky mother, Ruth Gordon.

Continental Divide: The editorial offices of the *Sun-Times* were home to columnist John Belushi.

Looking for Mr. Goodbar: Diane Keaton hoped to find him at the BBC on East Division.

The Blues Brothers: John "Joliet Jake" Belushi and Dan "Ellwood Blues" Akroyd drove around downtown Chicago in several madcap car chases.

The Hunter: Steve McQueen's last film involved a daring high-speed chase aboard a Chicago elevated train.

Will: Chicago native Robert Conrad portrayed Watergate criminal G. Gordon Liddy in this made-for-TV flick, which took in such scenes as the Westin Hotel's posh Consort Room.

Thief: James Caan and Tuesday Weld noshed at the Belden Deli.

Both the "American Dream" and "Chicago Story" TV series were shot on location in and around Chicago's neighborhoods.

THE SILVER SCREEN

The first movie studio in Chicago was built in 1907 at the corner of Byron Street and Western Avenue, the Selig Polyscope Company.

The best-selling novel and film, *The Towering Inferno*, was inspired by a fire on the upper floors of the John Hancock Building as seen from the nearby Playboy Building by writer Frank Robinson.

The Rocky Horror Picture Show has been shown at the Biograph Theatre on North Lincoln Avenue every Saturday night since March of 1978. The cult film attracts viewers of all ages dressed in outrageous garb mirroring characters in the rock musical.

The rest of America marveled at Chicago's gangster wars when Hollywood sensationalized flower shop owner Dion O'Banion's murder in *Scarface*, starring Paul Muni, George Raft, and Ann Dvorak.

THE BRIGHT LIGHTS

The musical *Grease* was first performed in Chicago before it went on to the bright lights of Broadway and the movies.

The first theater in Chicago was built by John B. Rice on Randolph Street east of Clark in 1846.

The "Glorifier of the American Girl," showman Florenz Ziegfeld, was born in Chicago at 1448 West Adams Street.

The Blackstone Theatre, opened in 1910, was leased by the Works Progress Administration during the Great Depression. Unemployed actors were paid $95 a month to present plays for the public at reduced prices.

Chicago's Shubert Theatre opened in 1906 as the Majestic Theatre and operated as a vaudeville house until 1932. It stood unused until 1945, when it was purchased by the Shuberts and renamed the Sam S. Shubert Theatre.

The Apollo Theater Center, 2540 North Lincoln Avenue, was the first commercial off-Loop theater built in Chicago, in September 1978.

THE AIRWAVES

Two of Chicago's best-known radio stations were started by two of the city's most prestigious companies. The call letters of the stations provided built-in company advertising: The *Chicago Tribune* owned WGN ("the World's Greatest Newspaper"), and Sears, Roebuck operated WLS ("the World's Largest Store").

The comedy team of Amos 'n' Andy originated their first broadcasts over WGN on top of the Drake Hotel.

The trials and tribulations of "Little Orphan Annie" and her dog Sandy were first broadcast over Chicago's WGN radio. Arf. Arf.

THE BOOB TUBE

Soap opera creator Irma Phillips, a long-time Chicago resident, is credited with the birth of "The Guiding Light," "As the World Turns," "Young Dr. Malone," and "Another World."

The longest wait for tickets to any show in the history of the television industry is to the Chicago-produced "Bozo's Circus" at WGN-TV. With a waiting time of eight years, many people order tickets as soon as the baby arrives.

Six TV stations—2, 5, 9, 32, 38, and 44—transmit their signals from the John Hancock Building, as do twenty-five FM radio stations.

THE LAST LAUGH

Chicago's comedy showcase—Second City—was founded in 1959 in a former Chinese laundry on North Wells Street.

Gone, but Not Forgotten

Theirs are not the legendary names adorning buildings or on the tip of everyone's tongue. Nevertheless, they do stand out among the city's cast of characters for at least one unusual reason or another and earn a place in the annals of Chicago history trivia.

Jamestown had its Virginia Dare. Chicago had its Helen Hadduck, the first child born within the stockade of Fort Dearborn in 1836. She later became the wife of John DeKoven, founder of the Northern Trust Company.

Otto C. Lightner, known as "the Hobby King of America," once lived in a South Michigan Avenue mansion known as "the House of a Thousand Curios," jam-packed with items of interest taken from other historical dwellings throughout the city.

"Does she or doesn't she?" Remember that famous Clairol ad? It was created by Chicago's Foote Cone and Belding agency exec Shirley Polykoff, who never told if she did.

Among the most celebrated criminals in Chicago history was Herman Mudgett, who murdered more than two hundred people on Chicago's South Side in an elaborate castle filled with various tortures. He was hanged in 1896.

Need a reason to celebrate? July 11 is designated as Cap Streeter Day in Chicago to honor the ornery founder of the city's Streeterville District.

Hey, big spender! John W. Gates, founder of the American Steel and Wire Company, was nicknamed "Bet-a-Million" by the local press for his daring investments of huge sums of money on the stock market.

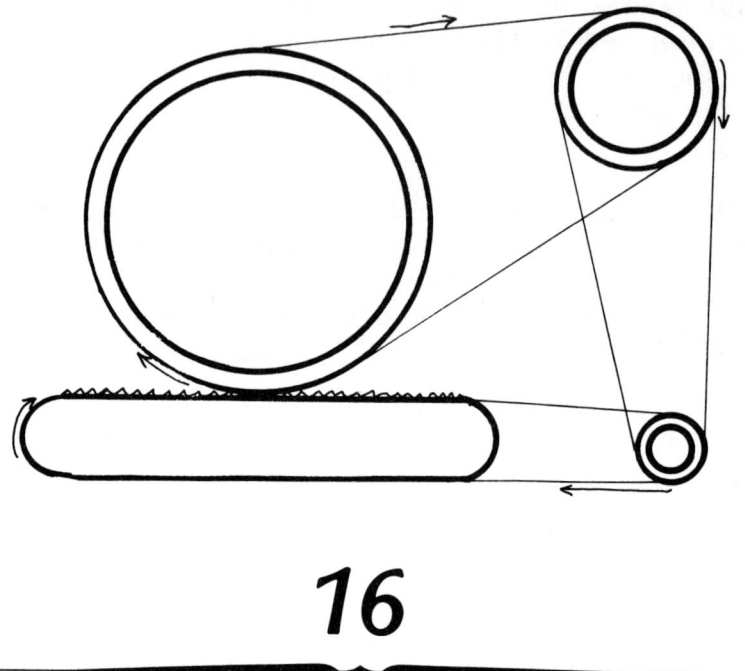

16

The Political Machine

Politics and *Chicago* are almost synonymous. And if things in Chicago are running smoothly, they do so because of the machinations that take place at City Hall.

With news from the political arena bombarding citizens daily from newspapers, radio, and television, it's just a tad impossible not to be a bit curious as to what they're doing down in City Hall.

MR. MAYOR

Bridgeport has been the home of more Chicago mayors than any other neighborhood: Kennelly, Kelly, Bilandic, and Daley.

Chicago's first mayor, William Ogden, founded the Chicago and North Western Railroad.

Mayor Richard J. Daley was elected to a record sixth term of office in 1975 and served the city longer—twenty years—than any of Chicago's previous sixty-four mayors.

Chicago Tribune editor Joseph Medill was elected mayor of the city in 1871, the year of the Great Fire. He ran on the "Union-Fireproof" ticket that promised the citizenry a fireproof city.

Chicago once had two mayors in office at the same time when the elections changed from fall to spring: The incumbent elected in the fall, Harvey Colvin, refused to relinquish his seat to Thomas Hoyne in 1873.

Like father, like son. Carter Harrison I and Carter Harrison II both served Chicago as mayors. Carter Harrison II was the first Chicago-born mayor.

Anton Cermak was Chicago's first foreign-born mayor, raised in Prague. He had once been a pushcart peddler on Chicago's West Side, collecting waste wood at industrial plants and factories and selling it as kindling to his neighbors.

MS. MAYOR

Jane Byrne is the first female mayor of Chicago, the first North Side resident to become mayor in fifty years, and the first mayor since Republican "Big Bill" Thompson to win the election without the endorsement of the Democratic party.

CONVENTION HOOPLA

Chicago has always been a convention city. A forerunner to McCormick Place was Chicago's "Wigwam," a huge meeting hall built for the Republican Party Convention in 1860 at the corner of Lake and Wabash. Abraham Lincoln received the party's presidential nomination here.

Those who supported Abraham Lincoln during the Lincoln-Douglas campaign were known as "the Wide Awakes."

Chicago hosted its first national convention of political importance in 1847, when representatives from the Northeast and the West convened to rebut President James Polk's veto of an omnibus rivers and harbors improvement bill.

Ulysses S. Grant was nominated to the presidency at Chicago's Crosby's Opera House at the Republican National Convention held in the city in 1869.

Franklin Delano Roosevelt was nominated for president of the United States in 1932 in the Chicago Stadium.

ELECTIONEERING

Of the state's 11,320 voting precincts, 5,407 are located in Cook County.

The first three voting precincts in Cook County were created in March of 1831: the Chicago Precinct; the Hickory Creek Precinct; and Du Page Precinct.

"Bathhouse" John Coughlin started the "endless chain" of voting, a fraudulent system whereby an unmarked ballot was secreted from the polling place, marked as a vote for Coughlin's candidate, and given to a hobo, who then went in to vote using the marked ballot and exiting with a fresh one, to be marked with Coughlin's candidate and given to the next hobo voter.

City elections in 1928 were known as "the Pineapple Primary" due to the number of bombs (or "pineapples") exploded during heavy gang warfare and the killing of "Diamond Joe" Esposito, candidate for alderman in the Nineteenth Ward.

BIG WHEELS/BIG DEALS

The consummate negotiator, Mayor "Big Bill" Thompson, settled the 1915 cable car drivers' strike by locking the disputing parties in his City Hall office until they agreed to accept him as arbitrator.

Chicago, Wisconsin? No, thanks, replied then congressman "Long John" Wentworth to a political deal proposing to annex the city to the state of Wisconsin.

96 THE CHICAGO TRIVIA BOOK

The land for Holy Name Cathedral, 730 North Wabash, was given to the Catholic church as a political payoff by William Ogden and Walter Newberry to get the Catholic vote for a bridge over the river at Clark Street.

POLITICAL FIRSTS

Chicago's first City Hall was located in the Saloon Building on the southeast corner of Clark and Lake streets.

Chicago was the first city in the United States to completely incinerate its refuse instead of dumping raw garbage into open landfill, beginning in 1971.

One of the first services provided the citizenry by city fathers, about 1833, was a free ferry across the Chicago River at Dearborn Street.

Chicago's first black ward committeeman was Edward H. Wright; Oscar De Priest was the city's first black alderman.

John Jones, a tailor by trade, was the first black holder of an elective office in Cook County, serving as county commissioner in 1871.

FORWARDING ADDRESS

Chicago's City Hall had seven different locations prior to settling into today's building on LaSalle Street in 1911, designed by architects Holabird and Roche.

17

Big Business

The business atmosphere in Chicago is intense, thriving, and competitive. The driving force behind the growth of industry in the Windy City was hundreds of determined and spirited entrepreneurs who heeded Horace Greeley's advice to "Go West" but who went no further than Chicago to set down business roots.

The men and women who sold everything from hardware to women's lingerie and invented anything from an electric saw to caramelized popcorn laid the foundation for many of the companies today that are not only respected citywide, but renowned in the national and world business communities as well.

I'M FOREVER BLOWING BUBBLES

Before the premiere of Wrigley's Juicy Fruit gum in 1893, William Wrigley, king of the chewing gum empire, manufactured soap.

Chewing gum magnate Wrigley started the incentive system of distributing premium gifts as an inducement for dealers to buy his product.

No small direct-mail marketing feat! William Wrigley promoted his spearmint-flavored chewing gum by mailing four sample sticks of the gum to each of the 1.5 million names listed in U.S. telephone books in 1915.

The Wrigley company introduced a candy-coated gum in 1921, P.K., which took its name from the gum's slogan, "Packed Tight—Kept Right." During World War II, Wrigley produced Orbit chewing gum but refused to identify it with a Wrigley label because rationing forced the use of inferior ingredients.

BUSINESS FIRSTS

Chicago is a shopper's paradise, and John McGarvin has the distinction of being the first merchant on State Street. He sold water for a dime a barrel in 1834.

Chicago's Wrigley Company was the first U.S. manufacturer to give its employees Saturday and Sunday as days off.

The first portable electric handsaw was manufactured in Chicago. The "Skilsaw" was developed by New Orleans inventor Edmond Michel to help cut sugarcane stalks.

Chicago's first business executive was Jean-Baptiste Point du Sable, who ran a trading post at Dearborn and South Water streets. Du Sable eventually sold the post to trader and silversmith John Kinzie.

The first brewery was constructed by William Lill and Michael Diversey. It was called, appropriately enough, the Chicago Brewery.

The city's first mail-order business was established at Clark and Kinzie streets by Aaron Montgomery Ward and his brother-in-law George R. Thorne in 1872.

WINDOW SHOPPING

Six world-famous department stores have their corporate headquarters in Chicago: Marshall Field & Company; Carson, Pirie, Scott and Company; Goldblatt Brothers; Montgomery Ward and Company; Sears, Roebuck and Company; and Wieboldt Stores.

Levi Leiter was Marshall Field's original partner in his department store venture, but he sold out his interest before his name ever appeared on the business shingle.

State Street became the main thoroughfare of the downtown shopping district through the efforts of Potter Palmer, who bought three-quarters of a mile of property along the street during the 1860s and convinced prominent merchants to become his tenants.

THE MIDAS TOUCH

When Joseph P. Kennedy purchased the faltering Merchandise Mart in 1945, he turned it around into the largest wholesale buying complex in the country, with hundreds and hundreds of showrooms and 7½ miles of corridors. Kennedy bought the Mart for $14 million—sight unseen!

HIGH FINANCE

Honesty pays. The Continental Bank, the oldest financial institution in Chicago, lost all of its customer records not once, but twice, during its history: the first due to the Chicago Fire, and the second time when the Goodyear dirigible *Wingfoot* crashed through its skylight in 1919. Both times the bank relied on the honesty of its patrons to record their accounts. Continental originally opened in 1857 as the Merchants Savings Loan and Trust Company.

Chicagoans used "Wild Cat" money during much of the 1800s. Since the national banking system was not yet in effect, the value of private bank notes held by citizens fluctuated daily.

THE BIGGIES

The nation's single biggest advertising agency is also the largest tenant of the John Hancock Building—J. Walter Thompson.

One of the largest U.S. piano and organ manufacturing firms was founded in Chicago by W. W. Kimball in 1864.

Four of the five largest mail-order businesses in the world are headquartered in Chicago: Sears, Ward, Spiegel, and Aldens.

The world's largest ready-to-wear clothing firm is also headquartered in Chicago—Hart, Schaffner and Marx.

THE OLDEST

The oldest business firm in Chicago still in existence today is C. D. Peacock jewelers, founded by Elijah Peacock in 1837.

The oldest Chicago company continuously owned and operated by the same family is the Iwan Ries & Co. tobacco shop at 17 South Wabash.

You're never too old. McDonald's founder Ray Kroc was fifty-two when he began his Golden Arches operation. He bought the name and procedure for his shakes and burgers from Mac and Dick McDonald of San Bernardino, California.

PARTNERS

William Rand and Andrew McNally worked in the printing

shop of the *Chicago Tribune* before putting their heads and their names together to form their own book publishing firm in 1859.

The famous partnership of Sears and Roebuck began through a classified ad placed in the April 1, 1887, *Chicago Daily News*. Richard Sears, a telegrapher by trade, asked for a watchmaker to repair a shipment of damaged watches. His ad was answered by watchmaker Alva Roebuck. The profitable association that ensued proved that neither partner was an April fool.

Montgomery Ward and Company, founded by Aaron Montgomery Ward, originator of the mail-order business, originally placed a restriction on its clientele. Early advertisements advised Chicagoans, "We sell to out-of-town people only."

Cyrus Hall McCormick, who founded International Harvester, also pioneered the concepts of advertising, home trials, guarantees, testimonials, deferred payments, and mass production in Chicago.

Forty-one of America's Fortune 500 companies have their corporate headquarters in Chicago.

Between 1882 and 1888, baker Henry Piper built houses for his workers in the narrow brick passageway behind his bakery on Wells Street, along with a school, to establish "Piper's Alley," used since the 1950s as a specialty shop complex.

George Pullman began the era of luxury rail travel in Chicago in 1858 when he converted two Chicago and Alton rail cars into sleeping coaches. To ensure that he'd rest in peace when the time came, Pullman ordered that his body be incarcerated in concrete and steel reinforced with railroad ties in Graceland Cemetery to guard against grave robbers.

When Ignaz Schwinn opened his bicycle factory here in 1895, it produced twenty-five thousand bikes annually. Each ten-speed bike contains more than ten thousand parts.

18

Animals

The wildlife in Chicago isn't restricted to conventioneers partying on Rush Street until the wee hours of the morning. With two of the finest zoos in the world—Lincoln Park and Brookfield—located in the Chicago area, four-legged and feathered friends are in abundance.

LINCOLN PARK ZOO

The Lincoln Park Zoo has been open to the public free of charge since 1878, when the Lincoln Park Commission decreed that "whatever the animal collection in Lincoln Park might be, it should always be free to the public."

The zoological collection at Lincoln Park was started in 1868 with a gift of two pairs of swans from Central Park in New York City.

In 1890, residents of North Park Avenue petitioned to have the sea lions, wolves, and foxes removed from the zoo after an incident in which two sea lions escaped across Clark Street and into a nearby restaurant.

"Wild Kingdom" host Marlin Perkins originated the "Zoo Parade" TV series from Lincoln Park Zoo during the late 1940s and early 1950s. Perkins is one of the few people in the world to have survived a coral snake bite.

CATTLE CROSSING

Although it's unlikely that you'll see any cattle trotting down the Boul Mich, Chicago's Loop has its own cow path at 100 West Monroe Street. The land has been preserved as such through an 1844 deed from Willard Jones, who reserved the narrow alley so that his cow could walk safely to the watering trough.

The Union Stock Yards on the city's Southwest Side were once called "Packingtown." Three million cattle and sheep and five million hogs were slaughtered there annually.

With more than 25,000 cattle, 80,000 hogs, and 25,000 sheep in its holding pens at one time, the Union Stock Yards found it necessary to sell manure at the bargain price of ten cents a wagon load.

FEATHERED FRIENDS

The *Rookery* building at 209 South LaSalle was a favorite roosting spot for pigeons, and the nickname "Rookery Building" stuck.

In an effort to prevent migrating birds fom smashing into the windows, the crown of lights encircling the ninety-eighth floor of the John Hancock Building are darkened for several weeks each spring and fall.

OTHER CREATURES

They won't bite! The giant lions guarding the entrance to Chicago's Art Institute were designed by a dentist turned sculptor, Edward L. Kenrys, in 1894.

At the turn of the century, sheep were allowed to graze in the Chicago parks to keep the grass mowed.

The Brookfield Zoo offered visitors the first dolphin show within the inland United States in 1961.

A Fish Fans Club was founded at Belmont Harbor in 1922 by Mayor Bill Thompson "to urge and encourage the propagation of fish in American waters."

19

Athletes' Feats

If the number of joggers running through Lincoln Park every morning is any indication, Chicago places a high priority on keeping in shape.

While most Chicagoans keep active for sport, a small percentage play sports for money. Many legendary names played ball in Chicago, where the fans are enthusiastic as long as the team is capable of bringing home the pennant or the loving cup.

THE GRIDIRON

The Chicago Bears officially received that moniker in 1922. The team was organized in 1920 by George Halas as the Decatur Staleys and the following year was known as the Chicago Staleys. A. E. Staley was the Decatur, Illinois, corn products businessman who commissioned Halas to start the independent football team.

Bears owner George Halas held a bat before he held a pigskin. He played briefly for the New York Yankees before a hip injury shortened his baseball career and he turned his attention to football.

The Chicago Bears were the first football team in the country to:

practice daily
take game movies to study their moves for strategy
have their own team band
have their own team song
publish and distribute a club newspaper
broadcast games over the radio
have a homecoming dinner for all ex-Bears
issue player diplomas

Founder and coach of the Chicago Bears for forty years, George Halas organized the American Professional Football Association in 1920, the direct forerunner of the National Football League.

Chicago is the only city to have an unbroken relationship with the NFL—the Bears have been members since 1920.

In 1939, Halas was the first man to trade players for a first-round draft pick.

In 1940, the Chicago Bears introduced the T-formation to football.

The Bears were featured in the first coast-to-coast radio broadcast of a pro football game, the 1940 play-off against the Redskins—72 to 0 in the Bears' favor.

The Bears' longest winning streak was thirty games without defeat, from 1932 to 1933.

The Bears once had to contend with a rival team also headquartered in the city, the Chicago Cardinals, coached by Jim Conzelman.

The first 1,000-yard runner in football history was Beattie Feathers, a 1934 Chicago Bear. Feathers ran 1,004 yards on 101 carries.

Chicago Bear Gale Sayers set the NFL's rookie scoring record in 1965 with 132 points.

The Chicago Cards was the first pro football team to attend training camp—in Coldwater, Michigan, in 1929.

During the manpower shortage in 1944 due to World War II, the Chicago Cards combined forces with the Pittsburgh Steelers and went on to win five games.

In 1899, the University of Chicago became the first western school to defeat an eastern team in football: Chicago won, 17 to 6, against Cornell.

Amos Alonzo Stagg is credited with winning the most games ever at one college—244 games as coach of the University of Chicago football team.

University of Chicago coach Stagg is also the only College Hall of Famer to be recognized as both a player and a coach of football.

RUN FOR YOUR LIFE

Some notable America's Marathon records:

> The course record was set in 1980 by Frank Richardson of Ames, Iowa, at 2:14:04.
>
> Sue Petersen of League Beach, California, set the course record for women in 1980 at 2:45.

The oldest man ever to participate in the race (1981) was seventy-eight-year-old Ben Mostow of Skokie, Illinois.

In 1980, seventy-four-years-young Ida Mintz was the oldest woman ever to enter the annual America's Marathon held in Chicago, with a finishing time of four hours and forty-five minutes. Ida made the event a true family affair by having her son, daughter-in-law, and grandson run the race as well.

Burson-Marsteller

WATER BABIES

Jump right in, the water's fine! The annual Chicago River Marathon was a long-distance swim from Municipal Pier (now Navy Pier) to the Wells Street Bridge.

Olympic gold medal swimmer Johnny "Tarzan" Weissmuller was the son of a saloon owner on Chicago's South Side. His first job was as an elevator operator and bellhop at the Chicago Plaza Hotel. Weissmuller began his swimming career at the Illinois Athletic Club.

AND HE'S OUT!

"The Battle of the Long Count" occurred in Chicago's Soldier Field, September 22, 1927, when Gene Tunney received an unexplained extended count (seventeen seconds instead of the usual ten) from the referee after being knocked down in the ring by Jack Dempsey. Tunney went on to win the fight.

KEEPING FIT 'N' TRIM

The first health and fitness club opened in Chicago in 1909, the brainchild of Viennese wrestler Charles Postl. He opened his first Postl Athletic Club, still in operation today, over Otto Roth's restaurant on South Wabash Avenue, convenient for dining patrons who felt guilty about overindulging.

Chicago Convention and Tourism Bureau

Need some exercise? Get a job as a runner on the floor of the Chicago Mercantile Exchange—they average between five to eight miles a day.

HOT AIR

The first U.S. balloon race left Dayton, Ohio, in 1876 for a destination outside the city of Chicago; however, no contestant even came close.

HOOPSTERS

The world-famous Harlem Globetrotters got their start in Chicago as "the Savoy Big 5," playing their first game at Chicago's Savoy Ballroom in 1926. They became "the Harlem Globetrotters" in 1927 and made their debut at Hinkley, Illinois.

SKATING ALONG

Winter sports enthusiasts in 1878 used locomotive headlights to light the pond in Lincoln Park at night for skating.

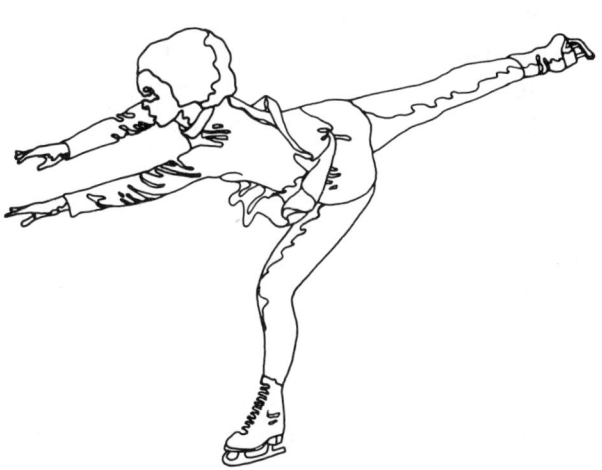

Once upon a time, Michigan Avenue workers could spend their lunch hour skating on the John Hancock Plaza ice rink, which was eventually abandoned due to the high cost of refrigerating the unit, excessive melting from the sun, high winds, and litter.

In 1922, Garfield Park was the site of the national ice skating championships.

In 1882, Chicago gave birth to a game called "roller polo"—hockey played on roller skates.

WATCH THAT PUCK!

Bill Mosienko of the Chicago Blackhawks scored a record three goals in twenty-one seconds in a game against the New York Rangers on March 23, 1952.

Bobby Hull scored the fifty-first goal of his career at the Chicago Stadium on March 12, 1966. The crowd gave Hull a seven-minute standing ovation, and the record stood unbroken for the next twelve years.

Blackhawks player Stan Mikita scored the first goal of his NHL career by having the puck ricochet off his body and into the net.

The Blackhawks endured a thirty-five-year Stanley Cup jinx put on by disgruntled coach Pete Muldoon, fired from his coaching duties in 1927. The Hawks finally broke the curse—and won the cup—in 1962.

THE GREAT AMERICAN PASTIME

Wrigley Field, at Clark and Addison, is the only major league ball park in America without lights for night games.

The Chicago Cubs, originally known as the "White Stockings," were nicknamed "the Colts" after manager Cap Anson's appearance on Broadway in 1896 in *A Runaway Colt*. "Cowboys," "Broncos," "Rainmakers" were other nicknames, but the "Cubs" moniker was coined by sportswriters Fred Hayner and George Rice in 1901 and referred to the team's usual practice of signing on young players—cubs—to replace the more proven players enticed away by the American League.

The Cubs was the favorite team of Chicagoland gangsters. Al Capone and his bodyguards were frequent attendees, always wearing suits—even in the hottest weather—to hide the fact that they were carrying guns.

Chicago Cubs groundskeeper Bobby Dorr pioneered the idea of keeping fresh baseballs in a wooden box buried near home plate instead of throwing them out from the bench.

Charles "Gabby" Hartnett, Cubs Hall of Fame catcher, was a teenage marble champion, winning some 55,000 marbles from competitors.

Stolen bases record holder Lou Brock began his nineteen-year career with the Cubs in 1961. Brock stole 938 bases.

"Gabby" Hartnett struck the famous "homer in the gloaming." When darkness fell on a 1938 Cubs-Pirates game at Wrigley Field, Hartnett hit the ball out of the park in the dark for a home run.

Mordecai Brown, who pitched for the Cubs between 1903 and 1916, was nicknamed "Centennial Three-Fingered Brown." Born in 1876, the year of the one hundredth birthday of the United States, he was missing two right-hand fingers due to a childhood mishap.

The Chicago Cubs, formed in 1876, is the only remaining charter member of the National League.

Chicago National League catcher William Schriver became the first player in history to catch a baseball thrown from the top of the Washington Monument, on August 25, 1894.

A black baseball team, the Chicago Leland Giants, was organized in 1907 by Frank Leland and Rube Foster, founder of the Negro National League.

"Babe" Ruth's last World Series homer occurred in 1932, when the "Babe" pointed toward the stands, then proceeded to hit the ball in the direction he had pointed—the Wrigley Field center field bleachers.

White Sox Park opened in 1910 (seating 44,492), Wrigley Field four years later in 1914 (seating 37,741).

Comiskey Park was named after White Sox club owner Charles Comiskey.

In 1979, disco dancing demolished the White Sox. They forfeited a game to the Detroit Tigers when an "antidisco night" demonstration led by local disc jockey Steve Dahl left the field unplayable.

Chicago White Sox owner Bill Veeck started as a Wrigley Field vendor, selling peanuts, soft drinks, and scorecards to the fans.

The Chicago White Sox, originally known as the "Invaders," were named the "Sox" by sportswriters Carl Green and I. E. Sanborn.

The 1888 Chicago White Stockings drew criticism from the *Sporting Life* weekly, which labeled the tight pants worn by the players as "positively indecent."

The Chicago White Stockings was one of ten charter members of the National Association of Baseball.

"Shoeless Joe" Jackson was one of eight White Sox players suspended from the team in 1920, suspected of throwing the World Series to the Cincinnati Reds.

20

By Land, Sea, or Air

Ever since the caveman invented the wheel, man has been looking for ways to move from one spot to another faster than his own two feet will carry him.

A key factor to daily life in Chicago is traffic—lots of it—whether by land, sea, or air. Quick access and easy transportation has become so vital to our daily comfort that we often take it for granted until budget crunches cut back on CTA service, or a heavy snowfall grounds the planes at O'Hare.

SOME FIRSTS

Chicago's first mass transportation line was established in 1859. It consisted of a horse-drawn street railway car operating on State Street between Randolph and Twelfth streets.

Chicago was the first city to have a rapid transit system running along a major highway—the West Side Subway opened on the Congress Expressway in June of 1958.

The city's very first subway was opened in 1943 and stretched for five miles beneath State Street. Engineers tunneled through waterlogged clay without a single cave-in.

THE CTA—FOR BETTER OR WORSE

Foot power versus public transit during rush hour on Michigan Avenue resembles a tortoise and hare race. The average CTA bus creeps along at three miles per hour, slower than the average person can walk in that same amount of time (4.5 miles per hour).

The Chicago Transit Authority was formed in 1946 from three privately owned transportation systems: the Chicago Rapid Transit Company, the Chicago Surface Lines, and the Chicago Motor Coach Company.

As of 1981, the CTA fleet consisted of 2,420 buses and 1,100 rapid transit cars, ridden annually by 643 million passengers.

The 1,100 rapid transit cars running on Chicago's elevated lines carry 150 million passengers annually over eighty-nine miles of city and suburban track.

The busiest bus routes in the entire city transit system are the #62 Archer and Archer Express routes, which carry more than 6,700 passengers during every rush hour.

The longest route in the CTA system is the #9 Ashland, at sixteen miles.

The bus route carrying the most buses is the #36 Broadway, with seventy-one buses on line.

TRAFFIC JAM

Settlers from the East traveled to Chicago in the nineteenth century in "Prairie Schooners," the name given the covered wagons pulled by teams of oxen.

Free horse and wagon delivery service from Marshall Field's store began in 1872.

The first stagecoach, owned by Dr. John L. Temple, left Chicago on January 1, 1834, carrying mail between Chicago and St. Louis.

The first stagecoach driver was John Caton, later chief justice of the Illinois Supreme Court.

Not all of America's autos were manufactured in Detroit. Chicago produced the Amalgamated Armac, Hertle, and Marble-Swift autos in the early 1920s.

Drake Hotel founder Ben Marshall built the first convertible automobile in the city out of a Packard.

Taxi! John Hertz founded the famous Yellow Cab Company in Chicago in 1906.

THE WILD BLUE YONDER

Chicago's first airport, the Chicago Municipal Airport, was opened in December of 1927. It was later renamed Midway Airport in 1949 to honor the Battle of Midway in World War II.

Midway was the busiest airport in the world from 1928 to 1959, handling almost 10 million domestic and 200,000 international passengers in one year.

Northerly Island, the man-made peninsula located south of the Adler Planetarium, once housed Northerly Island Airport, now known as Meigs Field.

O'Hare International Airport, originally known as Orchard Place, was named in honor of Lt. Comdr. Edward ("Butch") O'Hare, a World War II naval hero who gunned down five enemy bombers on one mission. Initially designed to handle 20 million passengers per year, it now welcomes more than 50 million travelers annually.

Nearly half of the more than 50 million passengers who arrive annually at O'Hare Airport don't even want to be in Chicago. They're simply passing through O'Hare on a connection to a flight for someplace else.

Every sixty seconds, two flights depart from or arrive at O'Hare Airport, which handles more than 131,000 passengers daily.

FLYBOYS

Up in the sky! It's a bird! No, it's a plane—the first airplane flight was flown over the city by Glenn Curtiss, who piloted a plane over the Hawthorne Race Track in Cicero.

Chicago Aero Club of Illinois member Octave Chanute was a glider pioneer who helped the Wright brothers in their study of aviation.

James Plew, a wealthy Chicago automobile dealer, was the proud owner of the first airplane in Chicago.

Charles Lindbergh piloted Chicago's first commercial airmail flight on April 15, 1925, from Maywood Air Mail Field to St. Louis and back.

THE FRIENDLY SKIES

The National Air Transport Company sponsored by Charles Dickinson, known as "the Father of Chicago Aviation," later became United Airlines, the nation's largest air carrier and the only airline based in Chicago.

In 1921, a same-day, round-trip flight between Chicago and Indianapolis in a giant six-passenger plane cost $125.

The nation's first aeronautical research lab was built in Cicero in 1911 by Harold McCormick.

McCormick also sponsored the first international aeronautics show in Chicago in 1911; pilots were paid two dollars for every minute they could remain airborne.

THE PLANE THAT NEVER FLEW

The *American Defender,* a monoplane that cost millionaire Charles Dickinson $17,500 to build, was rejected as a late entry in the 1912 Gordon Bennett speed race held in Chicago. The plane was left to virtually fall apart over the next several years without ever being airborne.

THE WATERWAYS

Long before the era of water pollution, Lake Michigan was first known as "the Lake of the Stinking Water." Residents living along the lakefront were known as "Puants" or "Stinkers" because they claimed to have migrated from a salt sea in the north.

Chicago Convention and Tourism Bureau

The first bridge was built across the south branch of the Chicago River in 1832, paid for in part by money from the Potawatomi Indians.

The Chicago River flows backward toward the Mississippi, thanks to the engineering genius of Ellis S. Chesbrough, the city's first chief engineer. To reverse the river's flow, a twenty-eight-mile canal was built from the south branch to Lockport, known as the Sanitary and Ship Canal.

Chicago's only luxury excursion liner is docked at Navy Pier—the SS *Clipper,* which maintained cross-lake service between Manitowoc and Milwaukee, Wisconsin, for twenty-nine years.

NEXT STOP: SHOWTIME

The Chicago, North Shore and Milwaukee Railroad built Ravinia Park in 1936 so their city-dwelling passengers would have an entertainment destination to escape to during hot summer weather.

21

The Neighborhoods

Most everyone who now calls Chicago "home" was once an immigrant from somewhere else, or at least has ancestors who were. And the ethnic pride in the homeland is evident in the distinctive character of each of Chicago's neighborhoods.

The Neighborhoods

The backbone of Chicago's character is its melting pot of citizens. The city's neighborhoods are populated by Jews, Assyrians, Chinese, East Indians, Japanese, Koreans, Thai, Vietnamese, Italians, Irish, Swedes, Greeks, Poles, American Indians, blacks, Hispanics, Germans, Ukranians, Bohemians, Moravians, Slovaks, Croatians, Serbs, Slovenians, Montenegrins, Macedonians, and Lithuanians.

The people of Chicago live in no less than ninety-three neighborhoods:

Albany Park
Altgeld Homes
Andersonville
Archer Heights
Ashburn
Ashburn/Gresham
Austin
Avalon
Avondale
Back of the Yards
Beverly
Bowmanville
Brainerd
Bridgeport
Brighton
Budlong Woods
Burnside
Canaryville
Chatham
Chesterfield
Chicago Lawn
Chinatown
Clearing
Cragin
Dunning
East Garfield Park
East Humboldt Park
East Side
Edgebrook
Edgewater
Edison Park
Englewood
Gage Park
Garfield Ridge
Heart of Chicago
Hegewisch
Hermosa
Humboldt Park
Hyde Park
Irving Park
Jefferson Park
Kenwood/Oakland
Lake Meadows/Prairie
   Shores
Lakeview
Lawndale
Lincoln Park
Little Village

Logan Square
Longwood Manor
Maple Park
Marionette Manor
Mayfair
McKinley Park
Mont Clare
Morgan Park
Mount Greenwood
Near North
Near South Side
Near West Side
North Center
North Park/Hollywood Park
North Town
Norwood Park
Park Manor
Peterson Woods
Pilsen
Portage Park
Pullman
Ravenswood
Rogers Park
Roseland
Sauganash
Scottsdale
South Chicago
South Deering
South Lawndale
South Shore
Stony Island Heights
Taylor Street
The Island
Uptown
Washington Heights
Washington Park
West Chesterfield
West Elsdon
West Englewood
West Garfield Park
West Lawn
West Pullman
West Rogers Park
West Town
Wicker Park
Woodlawn

22
What's Cooking in Chicago Kitchens

Were it not for the culinary genius and ingenuity of Chicago cooks, the tastebuds of the rest of the world wouldn't be savoring crepes suzette, stuffed pizza, caramels, Cracker Jacks, and numerous other confections that first appeared on the market in America's Second City.

130 THE CHICAGO TRIVIA BOOK

SOUP'S ON

Early settlers to Chicago just looked outside their cabin front door for dinner fixins: wild rice, corn, hickory nuts, maple syrup, blueberries, fish, deer, duck, and turkey.

CHICAGO'S SWEET TOOTH

The chocolate turtle, that yummy concoction of chocolate, pecans, and caramel resembling its namesake, was developed by Nicholas Johnson at his State and Wacker candy store in 1918.

The oldest candy maker in the city is eighty-five-year-old Martha Davis, a dipper who has been with Margie's Candies, 1960 North Western Avenue, since its doors opened in 1916. Martha is no doubt one of the sweetest ladies in Chicago.

The yellow brick factory of the Goelitz Candy Company in north Chicago produced more than 2 million pounds of jelly beans in 1981; its famous Jelly Bellys are a favorite of the Reagan administration.

The Baby Ruth candy bar was born in Chicago. It was named not for the famous ballplayer, as many people think, but for President Grover Cleveland's new daughter, "Baby Ruth."

If you smell chocolate in downtown Chicago, it's not your imagination. The fragrant pollution comes from the Blommer Chocolate Company at 600 West Kinzie and M. J. "Milk Duds" Holloway and Company at 308 West Ontario.

Brothers Louis and S. W. Rueckheim caramelized popcorn and peanuts in 1896 to invent Cracker Jack. True to its slogan, "The more you eat, the more you want," it sold 60 million boxes by 1920 and 500 million by the mid-1970s.

Necessity is the mother of invention. Laws forbidding the sale of sodas on Sunday prompted William Garwood to invent the ice cream sundae in Evanston in 1875.

Marshall Field's unique Frango mint recipe was acquired when it purchased the Frederick & Nelson Company, a Seattle department store, in 1921. "Franco," the abbreviated name for the store, was changed to "Frango" when the name Franco, the same as the Spanish dictator, became unpopular during the Spanish Civil War.

The only place in the world where the seven varieties of Frango mints are made is the thirteenth-floor candy kitchen of the Marshall Field's State Street Store.

A TABLE FOR TWO

Hotelier Ernie Byfield was inspired to create the Pump Room restaurant in 1938 after reading *Monsieur Beauclaire,* a romance written by Booth Tarkington.

Chicago Convention and Tourism Bureau

The four restaurants operated by Davre's Inc. in the John Hancock Center serve approximately one and a half million meals annually, averaging 15,800 customers daily.

Crooner Frank "My Kind of Town" Sinatra is so hooked on barbecued baby back ribs from Twin Anchors Tavern, 1655 North Sedgwick, that he has them sent to him by air freight all over the country.

The Berghoff, the landmark German restaurant on Adams Street, boasted an all-male bar until 1967, when women decided it was about time they stand and drink with the men.

Comedian Jack Benny once ordered ice cubes flambé at the Pump Room, noting that the posh eatery "served everything on a flaming sword except the check!"

You may be able to stump the waitress by walking into a restaurant and ordering a "Michigan straight on the rocks"—you'll be asking for a glass of ice water.

Lawry's Restaurant at 100 East Ontario was originally the Kungsholm Restaurant, world famous for offering its lunch and dinner guests miniature grand opera performances while they ate. The Kungsholm puppets, which performed such classics as *Tosca, La Bohème,* and *Carmen,* are now housed at the Museum of Science and Industry.

Adolph Renucci was the first restaurateur of Rush Street with his namesake restaurant, Adolph's, which opened during the 1920s and closed in 1981. Singer Bette Midler ate there gratis during the lean days of her career when she was performing at Mister Kelly's.

One of the most frequent diners at the Drake Hotel's Cape Cod Room was crooner Bing Crosby.

The first McDonald's was constructed at 400 Lee Street, Des Plaines, and opened April 15, 1955.

Each year more than two thousand students, franchisers, and managers graduate from McDonald's Hamburger University in Elk Grove Village to receive the bachelor of hamburgerology degree.

NOBODY DOESN'T LIKE SARA LEE

Baker Charles Lubin created the famous Sara Lee cheesecake in 1949, patterned after a cake he tasted at Chasen's Restaurant in California. The kitchens of Sara Lee are located in Deerfield, Illinois.

Forget the diet! The Sara Lee Kitchens in Deerfield use 27,000 pounds of whipping cream daily in preparing cakes, pies, and other calorie-laden goodies. What a shopping list for Sara Lee bakers, who also use, every year:

    3,000 gallons of milk
117,000 pounds of flour
196,000 pounds of butter
116,000 pounds of pumpkin pie filling
 40,000 pounds of cream topping
       8 million pounds of cream cheese

11 million pounds of icing
2 million pounds of sour cream

The Chicago Bears could play a football game in Sara Lee's four-story holding freezer, which is as large as a football field and can hold up to 8 million cakes.

MORE CALORIES

Just the thing for a hot summer day. Baskin-Robbins 31 Flavors was founded by Chicago native Burt Baskin. There are 110 stores in the Chicago area and 1,800 worldwide.

During the national shortage of eggs and vegetable oil during World War II, Chicago-produced Kraft Miracle Whip and cocoa were used as substitute ingredients, resulting in the famous mayonnaise or "salad dressing" cake.

Henri Charpentier, founder of the landmark Café de Paris on North Dearborn, invented crepes suzette while preparing a special dish for the Prince of Wales, soon to be Edward VII. The identity of "Suzette" is uncertain.

The Henry Piper Bakery on Wells Street, site of today's Piper's Alley, once employed more than five hundred workers and exported its goods to thirty-nine states. The bakery, which opened around 1870, closed after sixty years.

Mary Dunbar and Nancy Martin are fictitious women, but they are big money makers as names of food products sold at Chicago-based stores, Jewel and Dominick's.

CULINARY CREATIONS

Chicago chef Jules de Jonghe was the creator of Shrimp de Jonghe, the dish bearing his name.

Saganaki, a Greek specialty otherwise known as "flaming cheese pie," was invented by Chris Liakouras at the Parthenon restaurant in Chicago's Greek Town.

Betcha can't eat just one! More than 800,000 potatoes a day are fried into some 19 million chips daily at Jay's Potato Chip factory at Ninety-ninth and Cottage Grove. The plant packages fifty tons every day.

When it rains, it pours. A basic condiment found on every cook's shelf traces its roots to Chicago—Morton Salt.

Get your red hots! The hotdog was first sold at the 1893 World's Columbian Exposition in Chicago by Hungarians Samuel Ladany and Emil Riechl.

The first Chicago hotdog stand was built in 1938 by Henry Davis, known thereafter as "the Prince of Chicago Hotdog Stands."

Deep dish pizza? Definitely Chicago. And the deep dish variety was the brainchild of Ric Riccardo and Ike Sewell, owners of Pizzeria Uno and Pizzeria Due. Riccardo brought back the famous recipe after a tour of Italy in 1943.

LIBATIONS

A popular refreshment during the World's Fair of 1893 was whole watermelon that had been spiked with a bottle of champagne and then allowed to age in the icebox.

Union League Club wine clerk Steve Kelley is credited with developing the Pousse Cafe Cocktail: a multilayered, multicolored drink consisting of red apricot cordial, brown crème de cocao, white crème de menthe, yellow Chartreuse, green Chartreuse, and cognac brandy.

Mogen David wine premiered in Chicago one year after the repeal of Prohibition in 1933.

A grocery bill in the 1830s might have looked something like this:
pound of beef—6¢
pound of butter—6¢
barrel of flour—3¢
one dozen grouse—$1.00
one dozen quail—37¢
carcass of venison—$1.50

FREELOADERS

Kohlsaats Saloon, located at State and Madison streets, introduced the gimmick of free lunch to attract customers to drink at the establishment.

CATERED AFFAIRS

Gaper's Caterers began in 1896 as an after-hours job for Prairie Avenue houseman John Gaper. It now feeds more than 150,000 people annually at parties and soirees in the greater Chicago area.

"Patrick" is the only caterer in Chicago with an unlisted telephone number. You'll need references if you want to contract the services of this "Duke of the Gold Coast and Lake Forest."

ONE LUMP OR TWO?

The first tea room at Marshall Field's store opened in 1890 with fifteen tables. It served fifty-six patrons on opening day.

EATING HABITS

Chicagoans developed an affinity for steak on their dinner tables due to the proximity of the stockyards and slaughterhouses, making prime cuts of beef readily available.

Chicagoans eat more buffalo fish—5 million pounds per year (96,150 pounds a week)—than any other freshwater fish.

HEARTY APPETITES!

No mere continental breakfast for this pair. To celebrate the opening of the World's Columbian Exposition in 1893, two descendants of Christopher Columbus, the Duke of Veraguas and his brother, the Marquis of Barboles, were honored at a ten-course breakfast on the morning of May 6. The menu included fresh oysters, olives, fried peppers, tomatoes and onions, eggs with rice, veal chops, chicken, sherbet, roasted woodcocks, lettuce salad, and strawberry shortcake with kirsch, all washed down with sherry, coffee, and cognac. Pass the Alka-Seltzer, please!

23

Law and Order

Whether on mounted patrol, walking the beat, or cruising the neighborhood in a squad car, Chicago's men in blue help to protect the law and preserve the peace among more than three million residents. It's an awesome responsibility, but one that is vital to keeping the pulse of the city steady.

Despite bathtub gin and bootleg whiskey, Prohibition had its share of success in the city. The Washington Home, a private hospital for alcoholics, was closed due to "lack of business."

The fourth largest security force in the state belongs to the First National Bank of Chicago.

Under Mayor Carter Harrison's rule, the city had 6,400 illegal saloons, 2,000 gambling houses, 900 brothels, and 3,325 policemen to keep law and order among 1,700,000 citizens. In 1981, Chicago had 12,334 police officers to keep the peace among its more than 3 million citizens.

THE MEN IN BLUE

Chicago organized its first formal police department during the term of Dr. Levi Boone, elected mayor in 1855.

Police officers in the early days of the city signaled for help from fellow officers with a device known as a "creaker."

Mayor "Long John" Wentworth designed the Chicago police badge made of leather in 1860; it was replaced in 1862 by a silver star.

The Chicago police force assigned its first women to duty as matrons on April 30, 1885.

The Chicago Murder Bureau was established as part of the police department in 1905, serving as a special division of the force using photographers to aid in solving crimes.

I SPY

Allan Pinkerton became the city's first police detective in 1850 and eventually organized his own private agency, symbolized by a huge eye over the door and the words, "We Never Sleep."

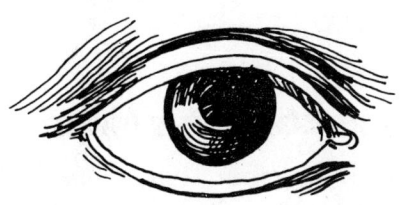

The first detective force in the city was formed in 1860 to help in getting to the bottom of unsolved crimes.

Chicagoan Kate Warn is credited with being America's first woman detective. She's buried in the city's Graceland Cemetery.

THREE ALARMERS

The Washington Volunteers was Chicago's first fire company, pledged to protect the city and led by fire warden Benjamin Jones.

The "Fire Bucket" ordinance of 1835 required every store owner to have "one good painted leather fire bucket" located next to every fireplace or stove in the building in case of emergency.

The Citizens Fire Brigade of Chicago, formed in 1857 after a fire in which twenty-three lives were lost, was composed of businessmen and insurance companies committed to removing valuables from burning buildings and preventing water damage and looting.

The first three fire engines in the city, named *Long John*, *Liberty*, and *Economy*, were purchased by Maj. John Wentworth.

HERE COMES THE JUDGE

In December 1980, Susan Getzendanner became the first woman to sit on the federal bench in Chicago. Getzendanner is a corporate lawyer and graduate of Loyola Law School.

ETC.

Despite its colorful and crime-ridden history, the Second City doesn't even have a place on the FBI's current list of the thirty most crime-ridden cities in the country.

The slogan "I'd walk a mile for a Camel" might also include going to jail in the 1880s, when it was still possible to be arrested on a disorderly conduct charge for smoking cigarettes on the street.

24

Some Windy City Weather

As the old saying goes, "If you don't like Chicago's weather, just wait twenty minutes!" Just about anything is bound to happen in the Windy City when it comes to meteorology.

Wind chill factors and snow (lots of it) are staples of any Chicago winter, balanced by hot, humid summer days that offer the perfect excuse to get out and enjoy the lakefront.

THE CHICAGO TRIVIA BOOK

HOLD ONTO YOUR HAT

With an average annual wind velocity of 14 miles per hour, Chicago is ranked the 39th windiest city in America by the U.S. Weather Service.

Tornadoes have struck the Chicago area three times in the last sixty-two years; in 1920, 1967, and 1976.

LET IT SNOW, LET IT SNOW, LET IT SNOW

The greatest snowfall (continuous snowing) in twenty-four hours occurred January 26 and 27, 1967, 19.8 inches.

The greatest snowstorm dropped 23 inches, total, on the city during January 26 and 27, 1967.

The greatest accumulation of snow was 29 inches of the white stuff on January 14, 1979.

The greatest seasonal total of snowfall occurred in 1977–1978, with 82.3 inches.

The least seasonal total of snowfall was during 1920–1921, with a measly 9.8 inches to shovel.

The greatest snowfall in one calendar year occurred in 1967, with 68.5 inches.

The least snowfall in any one calendar year was 8.3 inches in 1922.

The greatest snowfall in one month fell during January of 1918, with 42.5 inches.

The earliest measurable snow was 0.2 inches on October 18, 1972.

The latest measurable snow was 0.2 inches on May 11, 1966.

A RECORD YEAR FOR LONG JOHNS

The mercury plummeted to a bone-chilling −26 degrees on January 10, 1982, breaking the city's all-time record for cold temperatures of −23 set on Christmas Eve of 1872.

25

World Records

The biggest, the fastest, the best—Chicagoans have always been preoccupied with a bit of one-upmanship ever since their bragging about the World's Columbian Exposition of 1893 earned them the nickname "windy" for their constant boasting about everything the fair had to offer.

THE TALLEST

Chicago's skyline boasts the world's tallest, fourth-tallest, and fifth-tallest buildings: the Sears Tower (110 stories, 1,454 feet), the Standard Oil Building (80 stories, 1,136 feet), and the John Hancock Building (96 stories, 1,127 feet).

The First National Bank of Chicago knows something about "high" finance. It's the tallest bank building in the world.

You can go for a high dive in the forty-fourth floor swimming pool in the John Hancock Building, the highest in the world at 546 feet.

Chicago Convention and Tourism Bureau

The only restaurant where you can get lunch and a nosebleed at the same time: The Ninety-Fifth, located on the ninety-fifth floor of the John Hancock Building, is the world's tallest bi-level restaurant and lounge.

The Kemper Insurance Building at 20 North Wacker Drive, built by Samuel Insull in 1929, houses the Lyric Opera and is the tallest opera house in the world.

THE LARGEST

The Buckingham Fountain in Grant Park is the largest fountain in the world, constructed in 1926 and modeled after the Latona Fountain in Versailles. It shoots water a dazzling 135 feet into the air.

Although it's located one thousand miles from the nearest ocean, the Great Lakes Naval Station is the largest facility of its kind in the world.

Chicago's central water filtration plant, located on the lakefront north of Navy Pier, is the largest in the world.

The Chicago Post Office at 433 West Van Buren is the only postal facility in the world you can drive a car through.

Chicago was once home to the world's largest electric sign, which stood atop a building at Randolph Street and the Outer Drive. An advertisement for Canadian Club whiskey, it was destroyed by a wind storm in 1940.

McCormick Place, situated on Chicago's lakefront south of Meigs Field, is the country's largest exposition hall, the first hall to have more than 1.2 million square feet of exhibition space.

THE LONGEST

The longest dream on record, lasting two hours and twenty-three minutes, occurred at Chicago's Circle Campus on February 15, 1967.

O'Hare Airport has the longest commercial airstrip in the country, #32-L, a 12,000-foot runway.

THE OLDEST

The oldest ball park in the major leagues is Comiskey Park, built in 1919.

The Fifty-seventh Street Art Fair, held annually at Fifty-seventh and Kimbark in the Hyde Park neighborhood, is the oldest ongoing art fair in the Midwest, founded in 1948. More than eighty thousand visitors attend the two-day showing each year.

Chicago Convention and Tourism Bureau

ETC.

The world's smallest Bible, complete with the entire New Testament, is housed in Colleen Moore's $500,000 Fairy Castle in the Museum of Science and Industry.

The Riviera 400 Club at Randolph Street and Lake Shore Drive has the only swimming pool in the world covered by a geodesic dome.

The biggest tent supplier in the world is located in Northbrook—HDO Productions, Inc.

The John Hancock Building has the world's fastest elevator: it climbs ninety-six stories in forty-three seconds flat, fast enough to make your ears pop.

The first year-round children's zoo in the world opened in the Lincoln Park Zoo in 1959.

The largest indoor shopping mall in the world—all 191 acres, 231 stores, and 2,216,553 square feet of it—is the Woodfield Mall in Schaumburg.

The second largest carillon bell in the world, "Great Bourdon," is located on the University of Chicago campus, tipping the scales at 36,926 pounds.

The Shedd Aquarium is the world's largest indoor aquarium, showcasing 4,500 fish from 550 species.

The world's largest commercial book printer is headquartered in Chicago—R. R. Donnelley and Sons.

The Garfield Park Conservatory is the world's largest horticultural conservatory under one roof.

The Standard Oil Building is the world's tallest marble-clad structure, covered with 8 million tons of marble.

Buckingham Fountain is the largest fountain in the world, holding 1,500,000 gallons of water and pumping 15,000 gallons of water per minute through 133 jets.

The world's only chewing gum wrapper museum is located in the Wrigley Building. A rather well guarded company secret, it's closed to the public. Sorry.

The world's first service club, Rotary International, was born in the city in 1905.

The world's first singles organization was established in Chicago at the Fourth Presbyterian Church on Michigan Avenue. Founded in 1920 as "the Young People's Society," it became the Northminster Fellowship in 1932, nicknamed "Northies" and still a popular social organization for singles on the Near North Side.

26

Cocktail Party Tidbits

We all dread those initial moments when we walk into a room filled with people we don't know and fumble around for a conversation icebreaker.

Well, you won't have to fumble or mumble any longer at the next soirée if you walk confidently up to the first stranger you see and share some Chicago trivia from the following pages.

Cocktail Party Tidbits 153

Lettuce Entertain You Enterprises

Shoppers spend more than $150 million annually at Water Tower Place, averaging about $411,000 ringing into the cash registers daily.

The four stars of the Chicago flag represent Fort Dearborn (built in 1803), the Chicago Fire (1871), the World's Columbian Exposition (1893), and the Century of Progress Exposition (1933).

"Checagou" was first settled by French Jesuits in 1696, but the settlement failed by the year 1700 in the face of Indian hostility and was not resettled until 1779.

A diamond may still be a girl's best friend, but among the Field Museum's most prized jewels is the 5,890-carat Chalmers topaz, which weighed a whopping 10,200 carats in the rough.

New Year's calls were a yearly custom for nineteenth century Chicago ladies. The "beaus and gallants" of the day visited women at home to give their good wishes for the New Year. An empty basket hung on the door showed that the girl was not receptive to company; a basket decked out in ribbons and flowers indicated an open invitation for the men to visit.

John Kinzie, a silversmith by trade, was the only original settler of the area to be spared at the 1813 Fort Dearborn massacre.

The elegant Palmer House hotel housed a barber shop that had eight hundred solid silver dollars embedded in the floor.

The Hyatt Regency Chicago, the world's largest convention/exposition hotel, sits a few blocks from the site of the city's first hotel, the Sauganash Inn, operated by Mark Beaubien at Lake Street and Wacker Drive.

The popular children's classic *The Wizard of Oz* was written by Frank Baum and W. D. Denslow at Chicago's Fine Arts Building.

Graceland Cemetery, where many of the city's high and mighty are laid to rest, is one of the few memorial parks in the country to actually offer the visitor a map of the premises if you call or write ahead of time.

Warsaw, Poland, was officially declared "the sister city of Chicago" by Mayor Richard J. Daley as a goodwill gesture.

Ladies eligible for marriage were scarce in the early days of Chicago. Many young women from the East would spend part of the winter with married friends in the city, and a common question heard among bachelors of the day was "Do you know what young ladies are expected here this winter?"

The chrysanthemum is the official flower of the city of Chicago, prominently shown off at the annual mum shows held at the conservatories. It was so proclaimed by a City Council resolution in 1966.

Lincoln Park was created on the site of an old cemetery in 1869. The bodies of nearly ten thousand Confederate soldiers who had died in Chicago prisons had to be relocated to other cemeteries in 1870, and a smallpox hospital and a morgue at Dearborn and North Avenue were torn down to make way for the new park.

ANSWERS TO THE QUIZ

1. Ellis Chesbrough
2. Amos Alonzo Stagg
3. Garbage inspector of the 19th Ward
4. A sub-machine gun
5. A flower shop on State Street
6. Grant Park, made from landfill from the Chicago Fire refuse
7. The Ferris wheel
8. An illegal saloon
9. Gambler Mike McDonald
10. Drinking champagne from a lady's slipper
11. Cap Streeter Day
12. The Merchandise Mart
13. The caramel
14. Johnnie Weissmuller
15. World's Greatest Newspaper and World's Largest Store
16. The John Hancock Building
17. Comiskey Park
18. Kate Warn
19. January 10, 1982, −26 below zero
20. $150 million

Index

Academy of Fine Arts, 75
Ackroyd, Dan, 46, 86
Adams, John Quincy, 68
Addams, Jane, 13
Addison Street, 66
Addison, Thomas, 66
Adlai E. Stevenson Expressway, 63
Adler, Max, 71
Adler Planetarium, 71
Aldens, Inc., 101
Alta Vista Terrace, 60

Ambassador East, 21, 86
American Defender monoplane, 123
American Dental Association, 32
American Derby Races, 47
American Floral Art School, 38
American Medical Association, 32
American Steel and Wire Company, 91
Amos 'n Andy, 88
Anderson, Abra Prentice, 82

"Ann Landers" column, 51, 83
Anson, Cap, 115
Apollo Theatre Center, 88
Archer Avenue, 66
Archer, Col. William, 66
Art Institute, 75
Ash, Paul, 56
Ashland Avenue, 63, 68
Atlanta Rhythm Section, 45
Auditorium Hotel, 80

Balbo Drive, 66
Balbo, Gen. Italo, 66
Banks, Ernie, 38
Banks Street, 67
Barnett, Ferdinand L., 50
Baskin, Burt, 134
Baskin-Robbins 31 Flavors, 134
Batcolumn sculpture, 71
"The Battle of the Long Count," 112
Bauer, Julius, 57
Baum, Frank, 154
Beaubien Court, 67
Beaubien, Mark, 6, 11, 56, 67, 154
"Bedbug Square," 37
Bell, Alexander Graham, 2
Bellinger, Richard, 77
Belmont Avenue, 63
Belushi, John, 46, 86, 89
Benny, Jack, 132
Berdell, Nicholas, 8
The Berghoff, 132
Bertoia, Harry, 70
Berwanger, Jay, 2
Beyond the Forest, 55
Bilandic, Michael, 46, 93
Biograph Theatre, 18–19, 87
Blackstone Hotel, 83
Blackstone Theatre, 88
"Bleacher Bums," 38
Blind Pigs, 19
Blommer Chocolate Company, 130
Bloom, Ike, 19
Board of Trade Court, 62
Bogart, Humphrey, 84
Boone, Dr. Levi, 140

"Boss Town," 36
Boston Tea Party, 15
Boyington, William, 34
"Bozo's Circus," 89
Bridgeport, 93
Broadway, 63
Brock, Lou, 116
Brookfield Zoo, 104, 106
Brown, Joe E., 83
Brown, Mordecai "Centennial Three-Fingered," 116
Buckingham Fountain, 74, 148, 150
Buckingham, Kate Sturgis, 74
Bud Billiken Day Parade, 47
Burky, Frederick, 8
Burnham Avenue, 66
Burnham, Daniel, 42, 66
Burnham Park, 45
Burnside Street, 67
Byfield, Ernie, 131
Byrne, Jane, 94

Caan, James, 86
Cafe de Paris, 134
Calder, Alexander, 70–71
Caldwell, Billy, 6
Calhoun, John, 50
Canal Street, 66
Cap Streeter Day, 91
Cape Cod Room, 133
Capone, Al, 19–21, 23–24, 53, 115
Carmen Street, 67
Carroll, Charles, 65
Carrol Street, 65
Carson, Pirie, Scott and Company, 99
Caton, John, 121
C. D. Peacock Company, 101
Century of Progress Exposition, 9, 45, 78
Cermak, Anton, 62, 78, 93
Cermak Road, 62
Chagall, Mark, 70
Chanute, Octave, 122
Chappel, Eliza, 8
Charpentier, Henry, 134
Chase Avenue, 63

Chase, Blanchard, 63
Chauncey and Marion Deering
  McCormick Foundation, 74
Chesbrough, Ellis, 6, 124
Chestnut Street, 63
Chicago Aero Club of Illinois, 122
Chicago and North Western
  Railroad, 93
Chicago Bears, 108-9
Chicago Blackhawks, 114
Chicago Brewery, 99
Chicago Cardinals, 109-10
Chicago Coliseum, 34
Chicago Convention and Tourism
  Bureau, 34
Chicago Cubs, 115
Chicago Daily News, 51, 102
"A Chicago Decision," 38
Chicago Democrat, 50
Chicago Fire Academy, 77
Chicago Historical Society, 83
Chicago Leland Giants, 116
Chicago Limousine Service, 82
Chicago Lincoln Club, 39
Chicago Marriott Hotel, 26
Chicago Municipal Airport, 121
Chicago Murder Bureau, 140
Chicago neighborhoods, 127-28
Chicago, North Shore and
  Milwaukee Railroad, 125
Chicago Plaza Hotel, 111
Chicago Post Office, 148
Chicago Public Library, 14
Chicago Stadium, 94
Chicago Staleys, 108
Chicago Sun, 51
Chicago Symphony Orchestra, 56
Chicago Transit Authority, 120
Chicago Tribune, 27, 50, 88, 93, 102
"Chicago Typewriter," 18
Chicago Volksfreund, 50
Chicago weather records, 144-45
Chicago White Sox, 117
Chicago White Stockings, 2, 38, 117
Chicago-born celebrities, 84-85
ChicagoFest, 45-46, 54
"Chinamen," 39

Church Street, 63
Citizens Fire Brigade of Chicago,
  142
"City in the Mud," 36
Clarendon Avenue, 63
Clark, George Rogers, 65
Clark Street, 65
Clarke, Henry B., residence, 26
Clinton, DeWitt, 65
Clinton Street, 65
Clybourn, Archibald, 66
Clybourn Avenue, 66
Cody, Buffalo Bill, 82
Cohen, Mickey, 21
Colleen Moore's Fairy Castle, 149
Colvin, Harvey, 93
Comiskey, Charles, 117
Comiskey Park, 117, 148
Congress Street, 62
Conrad, Robert, 86
The Conservator, 50
Continental Bank, 100
Conzelman, Jim, 109
Cook County Hospital, 7
Cook's Saloon, 9
Cornell Avenue, 66
Cornell Drive, 66
Cornell, Paul, 14, 66
Cottage Grove Avenue, 64
Coughlin, "Bathhouse John," 39, 95
Cracker Jack, 130-31
Crawford Avenue, 64
Crawford, Peter, 64
Crosby, Bing, 133
Crosby's Opera House, 94
Crowley, Ruth, 83
Curtiss, Glenn, 122

Dahl, Steve, 117
Daley, Richard J., 93, 155
Daley Civic Center Plaza, 70, 74
Dalton, James, 8
Damen Avenue, 67
Damen, Rev. Father Arnold, 67
Dan Ryan Expressway, 62, 67
Dana, Charles, 36
Davis, Bette, 55

Davis, Henry, 135
Davis, Martha, 130
Davre's Inc., 132
Day Book, 51
Dearborn, Gen. Henry, 67
Dearborn Street, 67
"Death Corner," 37
Decatur Staleys, 108
The Defender, 47
de Jonghe, Jules, 135
DeKoven, John, 91
DeKoven Street, 77
de La Salle, Robert Cavelier, 65
Dempsey, Jack, 112
Denslow, W. D., 154
De Priest, Oscar, 96
Der Westen, 50
Dever, William, 20, 53
Dewey, Adm. George, 15
Dickinson, Charles, 123
Dillinger, John, 18-19
Diversey, Michael, 8, 67, 99
Diversey Street, 67
Division Street, 64
Dorsey, Tommy, 55
Douglas, Senator Stephen A., 14
Drake Hotel, 21, 84, 88, 133
Dummy Road, 63
du Sable, Eulalia, 6
du Sable, Jean-Baptiste Pointe, 6, 99
Dvorak, Ann, 87
Dyer, Dr. Charles, 14

Eagles Exchange Tavern, 6
Eastland disaster, 78
Eisenhower Expressway, 62
Ellsworth, Col. Elmer E., 15
Empire Room, 48
Esposito, "Diamond Joe," 95
Evanston Avenue, 63
Everleigh, Ada and Minna, 43
Everleigh Club, 43-44, 80

Fannie May Candy, 39
Feathers, Beattie, 110
Fenger, Dr. Christian, 7
Ferguson, Benjamin, 73

Ferguson Fund, 73
Fermi, Dr. Enrico, 38
Ferris, George W. G., 42
Ferris Wheel, 42
Field Foundation of Illinois, 74
Field, Marshall, 72, 99
Field, Marshall, III, 51
Field Museum of Natural History, 72-73, 153-54
Fifth Avenue, 62
Fifty-Seventh Street Art Fair, 149
Fine Arts Building, 75, 154
Finn, Mickey, 2
"Fire Bucket" ordinance, 141
First National Bank of Chicago, 140, 147
Fish Fans Club, 106
Fisher, Fred, 55
Flamingo sculpture, 71
Flanagan, John, 75
Floating Hospital Association, 33
Flora Hill disaster, 78
Foote Cone and Belding, 91
Fort Dearborn Massacre, 154
Foster, Rube, 116
Four Deuces Saloon, 19
Fourth Presbyterian Church, 151
Foy, Eddie, 78
Frango mints, 131
Franklin, Benjamin, 65
Franklin Street, 65
Freiberg Hall, 19
Friar's Inn, 45
Fullerton, Alexander, 66
Fullerton Avenue, 66

Galena and Chicago Union Railroad, 9-10
Gaper, John, 137
Gaper's Caterers, 137
"Garden City," 36
Garfield Park, 16, 114
Garfield Park Conservatory, 150
Garwood, William, 131
Gates, John W., 91
German Hospital, 33
German Sharpshooter Park, 48

Index 161

Germania Club, 39
Getzendanner, Susan, 142
Gherken, Heinrich, 8
Goelitz Candy Company, 130
Goethe Street, 37
Goldblatt Brothers, 99
Golden Gloves Boxing Program, 13
Goodman, Benny, 57
Goodwin, "Spider" Dan, 15
Gordon, Ruth, 86
Graceland Cemetery, 15, 103, 141, 154–55
Grand Avenue, 63
Grange, Red, 38
Grant Hospital, 33
Grant Park, 13, 26
Grant Street, 67
Grant, Ulysses, S., 94
The Grasshoppers, 40
Grease, 87
"Great Bourdon" carillon, 150
Great Fire of 1871, 76–77
Great Lakes Naval Station, 148
Greeley, Samuel, 60
Green, Carl, 117
Guardian Angel Mission, 11
Gunther, Charles "Candy Man," 34, 36

Hadduck, Helen, 91
"Hair Trigger Block," 37
Halas, George, 108–9
Halsted Street, 66
Halsted, William, 66
Halston Street, 82–83
Harlem Globetrotters, 113
Harmon, Dr. Elijah, 8
Harper, Lucius "Bud," 47
Harper, Richard, 7
Harris, Charles, 55
Harrison, Carter, 44, 78, 93, 140
Harrison, Carter II, 93
Hartnett, Charles "Gabby," 115–16
Hawthorne Inn, 23
Hayner, Fred, 115
HDO Productions, Inc., 149
Hefner, Hugh, 45

Heisman Trophy, 2
Hemingway, Ernest, 83
Henry Piper Bakery, 134
Hermitage Street, 68
Hertz, John, 121
Hesh, Frank, 34
Hilton, Nicky, 84
Hinsdale Street, 63
Hobson, Lt. Richard Pierson, 15
Hogan, John, 9
Holabird and Roche, 96
Holloway, Charles, 51
Holloway, Charles, 51
Holy Family Parish, 67
Holy Name Cathedral, 96
Home Insurance Building, 2–3
"Honky-Tonk, USA," 37
Hooker Street, 67
Hotel Atlantic, 39
Hotel Bismark, 39
Hotel Kaiserhof, 39
Hotel Metropole, 23
Hotel Randolph, 39
Howells and Hood, 27
Hoyne, Thomas, 93
Hubbard, Gordon, 8, 61
Hubbard Trail, 61
Hughes, Thomas, 14
Hull, Bobby, 114
Hull House, 13
Hutchinson, Charley, 75
Hyatt Regency Chicago, 36, 154
Hyde Park, 14, 66, 149

Illinois Athletic Club, 111
Indiana Avenue, 63
Indiana, Robert, 82
Insull, Samuel, 147
International Harvester, 102
Inter-Ocean, 51
Ireland's Restaurant, 18
"Irish Power," 39
Iroquois Theatre fire, 78
Irving Park Road, 66
Irving, Washington, 66
Iwan Ries & Co., 101

J. Walter Thompson Co., 101
Jackson Park, 14, 42
Jackson, "Shoeless Joe," 117
Jacobson, Walter "Skippy," 82
Jay's Potato Chips, 135
Jenney, Maj. William LeBarron, 2
Joel, "Piano Man" Billy, 83
John F. Kennedy Expressway, 63
John Hancock Building, 15, 26, 29, 87, 89, 101, 106
John Hancock Center 132, 147, 149
Johnson, Nicholas, 130
Jones, Benjamin, 141
Jones, John, 96
Jones, Willard, 105

Kaplan, Ahlyce, 3
Kearsarge Street, 67
Keaton, Diane, 86
Kedzie Avenue, 66
Kedzie, John Hume, 66
Kelley, Steve, 136
Kelly, Mayor, 93
Kemper Insurance Building, 147
Kenison, David, 15
Kenmore Street, 68
Kenna, Michael "Hinky Dink," 21
Kennedy, Joseph P., 100
Kennelly, Mayor, 93
Kenrys, Edward L., 106
Kerfoot, W. D., 77
Kimball, W. W., 101
King Edward VII, 81
King's Manor, 44
Kinzie, John, 6, 99, 154
Klein, Robert, 89
Kohnsaats Saloon, 137
Kraft Miracle Whip, 134
Kroc, Ray, 101
Krupa, Gene, 57
Kukla's Restaurant and Lounge, 44
Kungsholm Restaurant, 132
Kupcinet, Irv, 80
La Rabida Children's Hospital, 42
La Salle Street, 65
La Salle Street Baptist Church, 11
Ladany, Samuel, 135

Lady Elgin disaster, 78
Lake House, 45
"Lake of the Stinking Water," 124
Lake Point Tower, 28
Lake Shore Avenue, 63
Lake Street, 60–61
Lampmann, Heinrich, 8
Lauer, Kasper, 15
Lawrence Avenue, 66
Lawrence, Bradford, 66
Lawrence, Gertrude, 81
Lawry's Restaurant, 132
Lederer, Eppie, 51
Leiter, Levi, 99
Leland, Frank, 116
"Levee" district, 40, 43
Levine, Les, 75
Liakouras, Chris, 135
Libby Prison, 34
Lightner, Otto C., 91
Lill, Michael, 8
Lill, William, 99
Lincoln, Abraham, 94
Lincoln Avenue, 66
Lincoln, Mary Todd, 66
Lincoln Park, 16, 155
Lincoln Park Zoo, 3, 9, 104–5, 149
Lindbergh Beacon, 32
Lindbergh, Charles, 123
"A Line-O-Type or Two," 50
Little Giant, 55
"Little Hell," 38
"Little Italy," 38
"Little Orphan Annie," 88
Logan Boulevard, 67
Lombardo, Antonio, 18
Lone Star Saloon, 2
Loomis Boulevard, 66
Loomis, Horatio, 66
The Loop, 60
Lubin, Charles, 133
Lyric Opera, 147

M. J. Holloway and Company, 130
Mackin, Joseph "Chesterfield Joe," 8
"Magnificent Mile," 62

Majestic Theatre, 88
Manilow, Barry, 82
Marge's Bar, 19
Margie's Candies, 130
Marina City, 29
Marshall Field's, 4, 9, 27, 53, 99, 120, 131, 137
Marx, Barbara, 84
Mary Dunbar products, 134
Maxwell, Philip, 66
Maxwell Street, 66
Maxwell Street flea market, 47
May, Elaine, 89
McClellan Street, 67
McCormick, Cyrus, 37, 39, 102
McCormick, Harold, 123
McCormick Place, 94, 148
"McCormicksville," 37
McDonald, Michael Cassius "King Mike," 43, 53
McDonald's fast foods, 133
McDonald's Hamburger University, 133
McErlane, Frank, 21
McGarvin, John, 98
McKinley Park, 16
McNally, Andrew, 101
McQueen, Steve, 86
Mead Street, 67
Medill, Joseph, 93
Medinah Athletic Club, 32
Meeker, Arthur B., 11
Meigs Field, 122
Merchandise Mart, 26, 100
Merchants Savings Loan and Trust Company, 100
Mercy Hospital, 32
Merrimac Street, 67
Michel, Edmond, 99
Michelson, Albert Abraham, 13
The Midget Club, 47
Midler, Bette, 132–33
Midway Airport, 121
Midway Plaisance, 14, 42, 61
Mikita, Stan, 114
"Millionaires Row," 37
Miltimore, Ira, 33

"Miltimore's Folly," 33
Mintz, Ida, 111
Mister Kelly's, 133
"Mr. Sunshine," 38
Mogen David wine, 136
Monadnock Building, 6
Money, Eddie, 45
Monitor Street, 67
Monroe, Marilyn, 45
Montgomery Ward and Company, 99
Monticello Street, 68
Montrose Boulevard, 63
Moran, George "Bugs," 23
Morton, "Nails," 18
Morton Salt, 135
Mosienko, Bill, 114
Mostow, Ben, 111
Mudgett, Herman, 91
Muldoon, Pat, 114
Mull, Martin, 86
Muni, Paul, 87
Museum of Science and Industry, 42, 71, 132, 149

Nancy Martin products, 134
National Air Transport Company, 123
New York Lounge, 44
Newberry Library, 96
Newberry, Walter, 16, 96
"Nicholson pavement," 59–60
Nobel Prize for Peace, 13
Nobel Prize for Physics, 13
North Avenue, 64
North Michigan Avenue, 62
Northerly Island Airport, 122
Northern Trust Company, 91
Northminster Fellowship, 151
Northwest Expressway, 63

Oakley Avenue, 66
Oakley, Charles, 66
O'Banion, Dion, 18, 23, 87
Ogden Avenue, 65
Ogden, William B., 6, 65, 93, 96
O'Leary, Patrick, 8

O'Hare International Airport, 122, 148
O'Hare, Lt. Comdr. Edward "Butch," 122
O'Keeffe, Georgia, 82
Oldenburg, Claes, 71, 82
One, Two, Three Club, 44
Otto Roth's Restaurant, 112

"Packingtown," 105
Palmer House, 31, 154
Palmer, Potter, 7, 100
Parthenon Restaurant, 135
"Patrick" Caterers, 136
Peacock, Elijah, 101
Peck, Ferdinand Wythe, 56
Pein, Albert, 81
Perkins, Marlin, 105
Pershing, Gen. John, 66
Pershing Road, 66
Petersen, Sue, 110
Peterson Avenue, 66
Peterson, Peter Samuel, 66
Phillips, Irma, 89
Picasso, Pablo, 70, 74
Pieper, Pat, 53
Pine Street, 62
"Pine Town," 36
"The Pineapple Primary," 95
Pinet, François, 11
Pinkerton, Allan, 141
Piper, Henry, 102
"Piper's Alley," 102
Pizzerias Uno and Due, 136
Plank Road, 63
Playboy, 45
Playboy Building, 32, 87
Playboy Mansion, 33
Plew, James, 122
Polk, James, 94
Polykoff, Shirley, 91
"Porkopolis," 36
Postl Athletic Club, 112
Postl, Charles, 112
Powers, Johnny, 19
Prince Henry of Prussia, 80
Proctor, Barbara, 3

Proctor & Gardner Advertising, 3
Provident Hospital, 32
Pulaski Road, 64
Pullman, George, 33, 103
Pump Room, 81–82, 131–32

"Queen City of the Lake," 36
Queen Marie of Romania, 81
Queen Victoria, 14
Quincy Street, 68
Quinn Chapel African Methodist Episcopal Church, 11

R. R. Donnelley and Sons, 150
Radisson Hotel, 32
Raft, George, 87
Rand, Sally, 46
Rand, William, 101
Randolph, John, 65
Randolph Street, 65
Rathskeller Bar, 34
Ravenswood, 64
Ravinia Park, 125
Reagan, Ronald "Dutch," 83–84
Renucci, Adolph, 132
Reuben Street, 63
Riccardo, Ric, 136
Rice, George, 115
Rice, John B., 44, 87
Richardson, Frank, 110
Richardson, Hadley, 83
Riechl, Emil, 135
Riverview Park, 48
Riviera 400 Club, 149
Robin and the Seven Hoods, 55
Robinson, Edward G., 55
Robinson, Frank, 87
Rockefeller, John D., 82
The Rocky Horror Picture Show, 87
Roebuck, Alva, 102
Rogers, James Gamble, 33
Roman Catholic Eucharistic Congress, 11
Rookery Building, 106
Roosevelt, Franklin Delano, 94
Roosevelt Road, 62
Roosevelt, Theodore, 62

Index

Root, George, 57
Root, John Wellborn, 6
Rosenwald Fund, 14
Rosenwald, Julius, 14, 71
Rotary International, 150
Rubloff, Arthur, 62
Rueckheim, Louis and S. W., 130
Rush, Dr. Benjamin, 66
Rush Street, 66
Ruth, "Babe," 116

Saint Cyr, Father John, 11
Saint Mary's church, 11
Saint Valentine's Day Massacre, 23
Sally's Stage, 44
Saloon Building, 96
Sanborn, I. E., 117
"The Sands," 24
Sanitary and Ship Canal, 124
Sara Lee Kitchens, 133-34
Sauganash Inn, 6, 154
Savoy Ballroom, 113
Sayers, Gale, 110
Scarface, 87
Schmidt, Otto, 7
School of the Art Institute, 82
Schriver, William, 116
Schwinn, Ignaz, 103
Sears, Richard, 102
Sears, Roebuck and Company, 88, 99, 101-2
Sears Tower, 15, 32, 147
Second City, 89
Selig Polyscope Company, 87
Sewell, Ike, 136
Shedd Aquarium, 72, 150
Shedd, John Graves, 71
Sheil, Bishop Bernard, 13
Sheridan, Gen. Philip, 66
Sheridan Road, 66
Ship's Rail Bar, 44
Shoenhofer, Peter, 15
Shubert Theatre, 88
Sianis, Sam, 46
"Silk Stockings," 39
Sinatra, Frank, 55, 79, 84, 132
"Slab City," 36

"Smoke and Steel," 36
Sounding Sculpture, 71
Sousa, John Philip, 55
Southwest Expressway, 63
Spalding, Albert G., 2
Spiegel Company, 101
SS Clipper, 125
SS Iowa, 78
Stagg, Amos Alonzo, 2, 110
Staley, A. E., 108
Standard Oil Building, 71, 147, 150
State Street, 60
Stone, Melville, 51
The Store Saloon, 43
Stose, Clemens, 8
Streeter, Capt. George Wellington, 20, 64
Streeterville, 64
"Suicide Squad," 38
Sulzer, Konrad, 63
Sulzer Road, 63
Sun-Times, 51, 86
Surgical Science Museum, 33
Susan & God, 81

Tap Root Pub, 77
Taylor, Bert, 50
Taylor, Elizabeth, 84
Telephone Museum, 2
Teller, Archibald, 39
Temple, Dr. John L., 121
Thomas, Theodore, 56
Thomason, Samuel Emory, 50
Thompson, "Bill Bill," 15, 94-95, 106
Thompson, James, 59
Thompson, Lydia "Black Crook," 43
Thorne, George R., 99
Tiffany, Louis C., 4
The Times, 50
Todd Street, 66
Torrio, Johnny, 18-20
The Towering Inferno, 87
Tremont House Hotel, 33
Tribune Tower, 28
"Tulip Tech," 38
Tunney, Gene, 112
Tuskegee Institute, 14

Twelfth Street, 62
Twenty-second Street, 62
Twin Anchors Tavern, 132
Tyler Street, 62

Underground Railroad, 14
Union League Club of Chicago, 81, 136
Union Stock Yards, 105–6
Unione Sicilione, 18
United Airlines, 123
University of Chicago, 13, 38, 66, 110, 150

Wabash Avenue, 66
Wacker, Charles, 67
Wacker Drive, 67
Walkins, John, 7
Wall of Respect, 75
Ward, Aaron Montgomery, 13, 99, 101–2
Warn, Kate, 141
Washington, Booker T., 14
The Washington Home, 140
Washington Park, 14, 42
Washington Park Race Track, 47
Washington Street, 63
The Washington Volunteers, 141
Water Tower, 34
Water Tower Place, 28, 153
Watson, Carrie, 43
Weiss, Hymie, 21, 23
Weissmuller, Johnny "Tarzan," 111
Weld, Tuesday, 86
Wells, Captain William, 65

Wells Street, 62, 65
Wentworth Avenue, 65
Wentworth, "Long John," 9, 24, 65, 95, 140–41
West Side German High School, 10
Western Avenue, 61, 64
Westin Hotel, 83, 86
WGN Radio, 88
"The Wheaton Iceman," 38
White Stockings, 115
Whitehall Hotel, 3
"The Wide Awakes," 94
Wieboldt Stores, 99
Wigwam Building, 32, 94
Williams, Daniel Hale, 32
Williams, Dr. Henry, 2
Wilson Avenue, 66
Wilson, John P. 66
"Windy City," 36
Wizard of Oz, 54
WLS Radio, 88
Woodfield Mall, 150
Woods Charitable Fund, Inc., 74
World's Columbian Exposition, 42
Wright, Edward H., 96
Wright, Frank Lloyd, 25–26
Wrigley Chewing Gum, 10, 98–99
Wrigley Field, 115
Wrigley, William, 30, 98

Yellow Cab Company, 121
Yerkes, Charles Tyson, 53
"Young People's Society," 151

Ziegfeld, Florenz, 87